NEW JERSEY'S
DISTINGUISHED
RESTAURANTS

1 9 9 4

∽

Published by the Society of Quality Restaurants of New Jersey

---

Copyright © 1993 Society of Quality Restaurants of New Jersey. No part of this book may be reproduced, stored in a retrieval system, or transmitted in any form, by any means, including mechanical, electronic, photocopying, recording, or otherwise, without prior written permission of the publisher. Inquires should be addressed to Society of Quality Restaurants of New Jersey, 5 Wessman Drive, West Orange, New Jersey 07052.

Regarding corporate gifts, please call: 201 731-8548

ISBN 09634765-1-3

EDITOR: Larry Lazar

DESIGN: Frederick & Froberg Design Offices, Inc.

ART DIRECTION: William Frederick

PRODUCTION: Deborah O'Connell

PHOTOGRAPHER: William Tomlin, William Studio
and Michael J. D'Elia

COVER: Erich Lessing/Art Resource, NY
Vincent Van Gogh, Cafe Terrace at Night (Place du Forum in Arles, France) 1888
Rijksmuseum Kroller-Muller, Otterlo, Netherlands

Printed in the USA

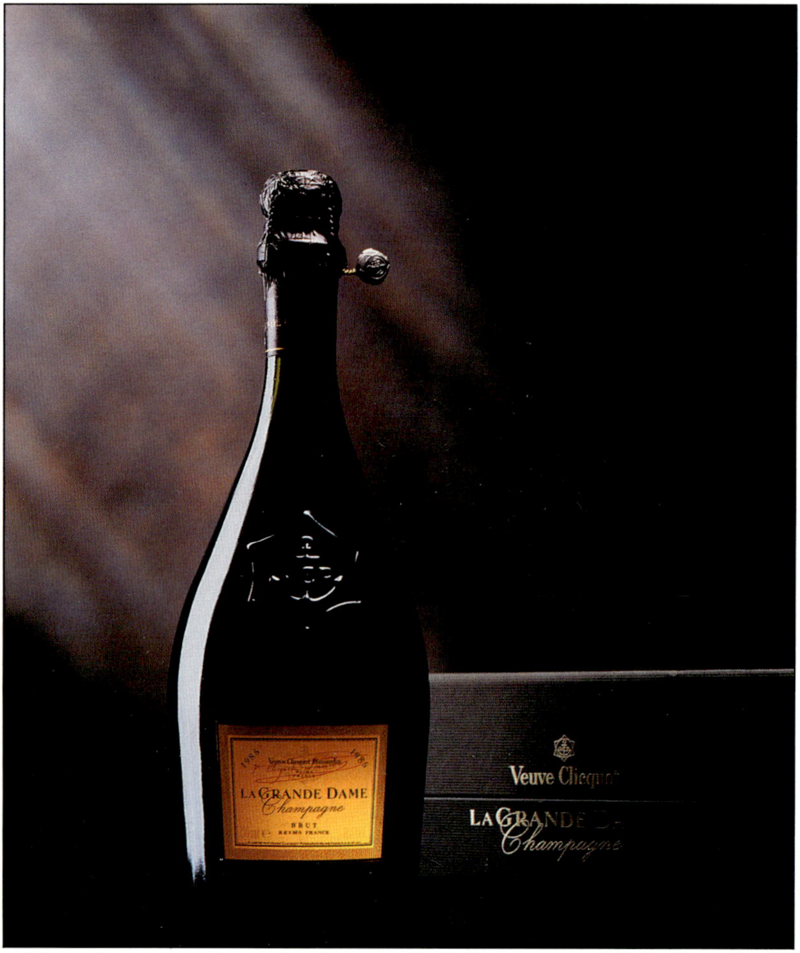

Table of Contents

Introduction	5	Il Capriccio	74
County Maps		Il Tulipano	76
Sussex and Warren	9	Il Villino	78
Morris	11	The Inn at Millrace Pond	80
Bergen, Hudson and Essex	13	Ken Marcotte	82
Hunterdon and Somerset	15	Knife and Fork Inn	84
Union, Middlesex and Monmouth	17	La Cucina Ristorante & Cafe	86
Mercer and Burlington	19	L'Affaire 22	88
Atlantic and Cape May	21	La Gondola	90
Restaurant Reviews		Lahiere's	92
Auberge Swiss	22	L'Allegria	94
Axelsson's Blue Claw Restaurant	24	Lantana	96
Beau Rivage	26	Le Papillon	98
Benito Ristorante	28	Llewellyn Farms	100
The Bernards Inn	30	The Manor	102
Black Forest Inn	32	Mattar's	104
Black Horse Inn	34	Old Mill Inn	106
Braddock's Tavern	36	Panico's	108
Chateau Silvana	38	Ram's Head Inn	110
Creations Restaurant & Meeting Place	40	Rod's 1890's Restaurant	112
Cucina di Roma	42	Rudolfo Ristorante	114
Dennis Foy's Townsquare	44	The Ryland Inn	116
Diamond's	46	Sammy's Ye Old Cider Mill	118
The Dining Room at The Hilton at Short Hills	48	Sestri Caffe & Ristorante	120
The Ebbitt Room	50	Sing Ya	122
Eccola Italian Bistro	52	Valentino's	124
The Farmingdale House	54	Villa Amalfi	126
40 Main Street	56	Washington Inn	128
Four Seas, Cuisines of China	58	**Features**	
The Frog and The Peach	60	"Choosing the Right Wine" by Tom Maresca	131
Fromagerie	62	Red Wine Wheel	132
Girafe	64	White Wine Wheel	134
The Grand Cafe	66	Gourmet Pantry	145
Harlequin Cafe	68	**Indexes**	
Highlawn Pavilion	70	Restaurants by Cuisine	158
Iberia Peninsula	72	Recipes	159

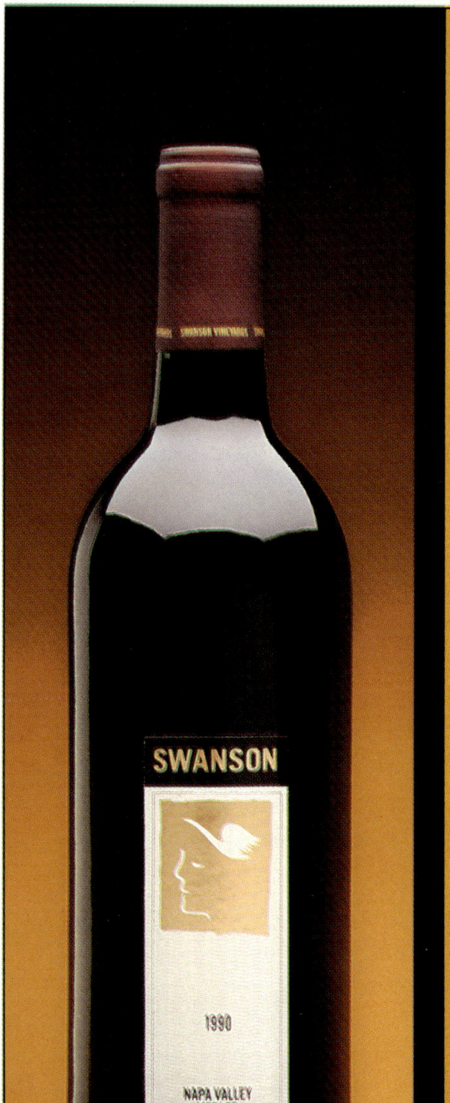

Introduction

With the influx of premier restaurants in the last decade world-class dining became a reality in New Jersey.

Restaurateurs created engaging dining facilities, staffed them with proficient professional servers and stocked their wine cellars with an extensive award-winning selection of bottles skillfully chosen to complement impressive cuisine.

Stellar chefs (many of whom are also owners) manage the kitchens of these serious dining spots. These culinary craftsmen – who previously distinguished themselves at celebrated restaurants in New York, California, France, Italy and China – were attracted to the Garden State because of its premier ingredients and the quality of life in New Jersey.

New Jersey's Distinguished Restaurants, 1994 was published to help you select restaurants where the management and staff devote themselves to providing patrons with prime quality dining experiences. The photographs and profiles of the restaurants were designed to allow you to choose which of these premier establishments suit your taste.

New Jersey's Distinguished Restaurants, 1994 also incorporates recipes of signature dishes from these prestigious restaurants so you can reproduce these delights at home. The recipes were tested in Gourmet's Executive Dining Room by Chef Sara Moulton and Sous Chef Lori Walther, preserving the individual style of each New Jersey Restaurant. A "Gourmet Pantry" section is also included with recipes and procedures (previously published in Gourmet Magazine) for preparing basic ingredients required in these signature recipes. In addition there are "Chef's Suggested Menus" recommending additional dishes to complement the signature dish.

The restaurants chosen to be included in the 1994 guide were limited to full-service establishments (allowed to serve wine with food). They were selected based on published appraisals by several restaurant critics, published polls of the dining public, a consensus of independent SQR auditors and the judgments of the editor (Larry Lazar, restaurant critic of Omnibus Magazine) plus a panel of experts chosen by the editor.

The restaurants in this book support SQR (The Society of Quality Restaurants of New Jersey, Inc.) – a company that develops, implements and manages total quality management programs designed to assist restaurateurs meet the expectations of their clientele. The core of the program is the acquisition of statistically valid feedback from independent "auditors" who volunteer to assess the quality status of the restaurants in this guide.

We are devoted to frequently evaluating New Jersey's distinguished restaurants, helping them maximize quality dining. In addition, SQR will continue to seek other full-service New Jersey restaurants that adhere to the basic quality tenets of providing diners with superior cuisine and wine served by skillful, attentive, cordial wait-staffs in clean, attractive surroundings.

Your suggestions of restaurants omitted from this guide that meet these criteria are appreciated. If you wish to suggest other full-service restaurants that weren't included, or if you would like to join this exciting quality audit program, please return the card enclosed in this guide.

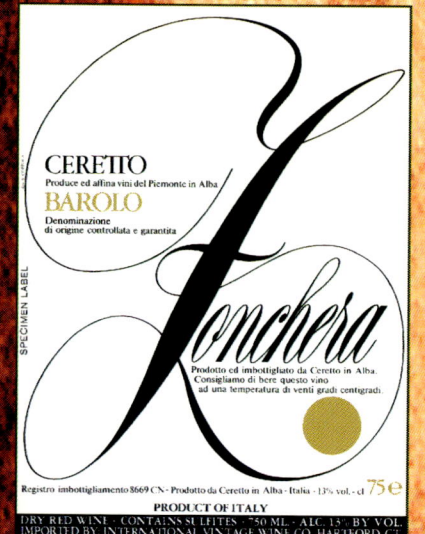

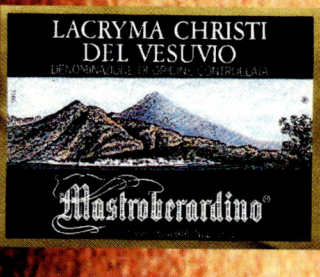

Fine Family of Wines

This book also contains an article to counsel diners on choosing the wine best suited to partner with food and their tastes. This essay, written by award-winning author Tom Maresca is included to add pleasure to your dining experience. For a more comprehensive work on choosing wines best suited for food in a wide variety of situations, one should read Mr. Maresca's "The Right Wine: A User's Manual" published by Grove Weidenfeld in 1990 (and available in a paperback edition by Grove-Evergreen books).

Mr. Maresca is also the author of "Mastering Wine" voted the "Wine Book of the Year" in 1985 and is a nationally known and internationally honored wine writer whose credits include *Attenzione, Food & Wine Magazine, Self, Town and Country, Ultra* and *Wine & Spirits*.

Bon Appétit!

Larry Lazar

To my loving dining companion and world-class wife, Naomi.

A fond thanks to quality appraisers, dining companions and friends Arthur and Paula Fruchtman and Lowell and Rosalie Saferstein; and to my son Jonathan – SQR marketing executive and perceptive dining companion – my loving thanks.

My appreciation and sincere *grazie tante* for all their support and efforts go to: Neil Barnett, Daniel Cannizzo, Diane Carr, Colette deChalus, Louis DeMarino, Antonio Grande, Genny Latour Huss, Peter Keller, Anthony Knapp, Harry Knowles, Kurt Knowles, Wade Knowles, Desmond Lloyd, Aldo Marsiglia, Arthur McGreevy, Sara Moulton, Frank Panico, Gregorio Polimeni, Alice Rochat, George Thierry, Lori Walther and Ken Woodin, plus all the unsung dining heroes in the SQR Appraisal Corps.

DINERS' ETIQUETTE

Reservations are an unwritten contract between diners and the restaurant. They help restaurants please patrons by minimizing wait times and assuring proper staffing. However, diners should live up to their side of the contract. Cancel immediately if your plans change.

New Jersey law doesn't require no-smoking sections. However, fine restaurants without separate sections have modern air cleaning equipment. Courteous smoking diners try not to inconvenience those around them that do not smoke.

Urbane restaurants that do not require jackets and/or ties for gentlemen expect patrons will dress in a manner consistent with a refined dining experience.

KEY

Reservations
Suggested

Non-Smoking Section
also Available

Handicapped
Accessible

THE MORE YOU KNOW CHAMPAGNE THE MORE YOU'LL LOVE BOLLINGER

" The best Champagne for the money if one wants a luxury cuvée of rich, toasty, creamy, flavorful sparkling wine.." wrote *Robert Parker* about Bollinger.

CHAMPAGNE
BOLLINGER
SPECIAL CUVÉE
BRUT

PRODUCE OF FRANCE

SUSSEX · WARREN

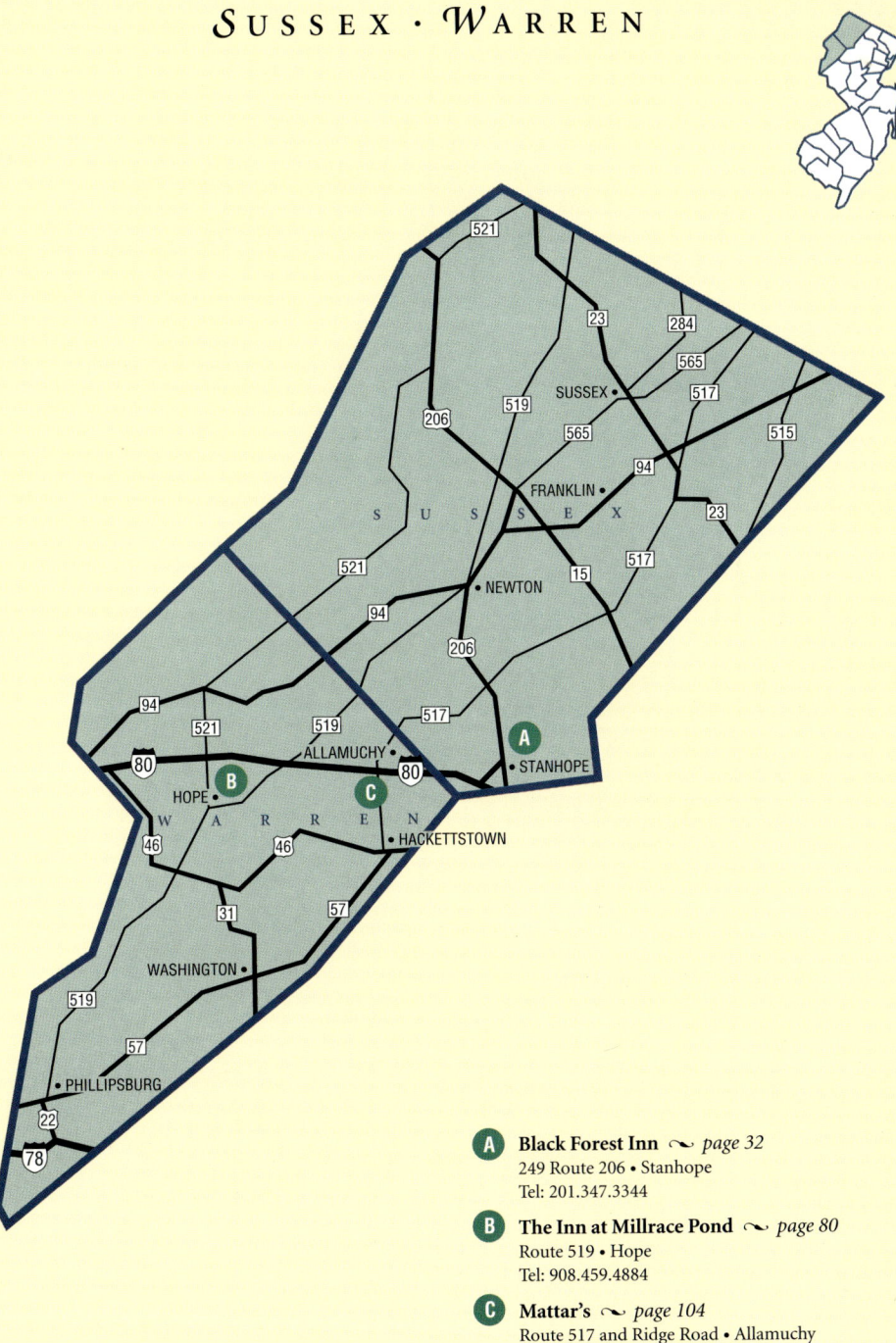

A **Black Forest Inn** ~ *page 32*
249 Route 206 • Stanhope
Tel: 201.347.3344

B **The Inn at Millrace Pond** ~ *page 80*
Route 519 • Hope
Tel: 908.459.4884

C **Mattar's** ~ *page 104*
Route 517 and Ridge Road • Allamuchy
Tel: 908.852.2300

Fruit Infused FINLANDIA

A fun loving people, the Finns decided to add some zest to thaw the frigid days when darkness covers their world. Some of their harvest fruit was added to their favorite Finlandia Vodka, producing a delightful taste sensation that brought a smile to everyone's face.

Today, this wonderful mixture is shared all over the world. The cold, clear, crisp, Finlandia Vodka infused with only the freshest of fruits. Fruit Infused Finlandia, a drink with a long history of great taste and good times.

MORRIS

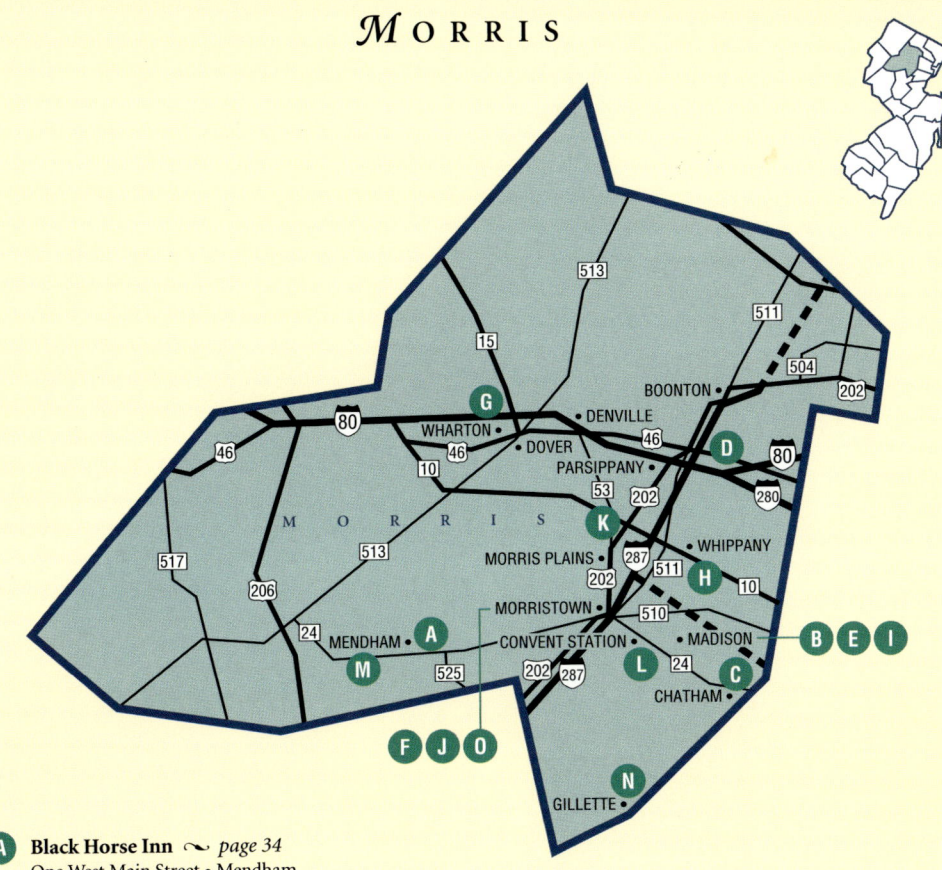

A **Black Horse Inn** ~ *page 34*
One West Main Street • Mendham
Tel: 201.543.7300

B **Creations Restaurant & Meeting Place** ~ *page 40*
54 Main Street • Madison
Tel: 201.966.0252

C **Dennis Foy's Townsquare** ~ *page 44*
6 Roosevelt Avenue • Chatham
Tel: 201.701.0303

D **Eccola Italian Bistro** ~ *page 52*
1082 Route 46 West • Parsippany
Tel: 201.334.8211

E **Four Seas, Cuisines of China** ~ *page 58*
24 Main Street • Madison
Tel: 201.822.2899

F **The Grand Cafe** ~ *page 66*
42 Washington Street • Morristown
Tel: 201.540.9444

G **Harlequin Cafe** ~ *page 68*
322 South Main Street • Wharton
Tel: 201.366.8154

H **Il Capriccio** ~ *page 74*
633 Route 10 East • Whippany
Tel: 201.884.9175

I **L'Allegria** ~ *page 94*
9-11 Prospect Street • Madison
Tel: 201.377.6808

J **Le Papillon** ~ *page 98*
142 South Street • Morristown
Tel: 201.539.8088

K **Llewellyn Farms** ~ *page 100*
Routes 202 & 10 • Morris Plains
Tel: 201.538.4323

L **Rod's 1890's Restaurant** ~ *page 112*
Route 24 • Convent Station
Tel: 201.539.6666

M **Sammy's Ye Old Cider Mill** ~ *page 118*
Route 24 West • Mendham
Tel: 201.543.7675

N **Sestri Caffe & Ristorante** ~ *page 120*
342 Valley Road • Gillette
Tel: 908.647.0697

O **Valentino's** ~ *page 124*
150 South Street • Morristown
Tel: 201.993.8066

BERGEN · HUDSON · ESSEX

- **A** **The Dining Room at The Hilton at Short Hills** ~ *page 48*
  41 JFK Parkway • Short Hills
  Tel: 201.379.0100

- **B** **40 Main Street** ~ *page 56*
  40 Main Street • Millburn
  Tel: 201.376.4444

- **C** **Highlawn Pavilion** ~ *page 70*
  Eagle Rock Reservation • West Orange
  Tel: 201.731.DINE (3463)

- **D** **Iberia Peninsula** ~ *page 72*
  69 Ferry Street • Newark
  Tel: 201.344.5611

- **E** **Il Tulipano** ~ *page 76*
  1131 Pompton Avenue • Cedar Grove
  Tel: 201.256.9300

- **F** **Il Villino** ~ *page 78*
  53 Franklin Turnpike • Waldwick
  Tel: 201.652.8880

- **G** **Lantana** ~ *page 96*
  1148 Paterson Plank Road • Secaucus
  Tel: 201.867.1065

- **H** **The Manor** ~ *page 102*
  111 Prospect Avenue • West Orange
  Tel: 201.731.2360

- **I** **Sing Ya** ~ *page 122*
  520 Sylvan Avenue • Englewood Cliffs
  Tel: 201.568.9855

- **J** **Villa Amalfi** ~ *page 126*
  793 Palisades Avenue • Cliffside Park
  Tel: 201.886.8626

Hunterdon · Somerset

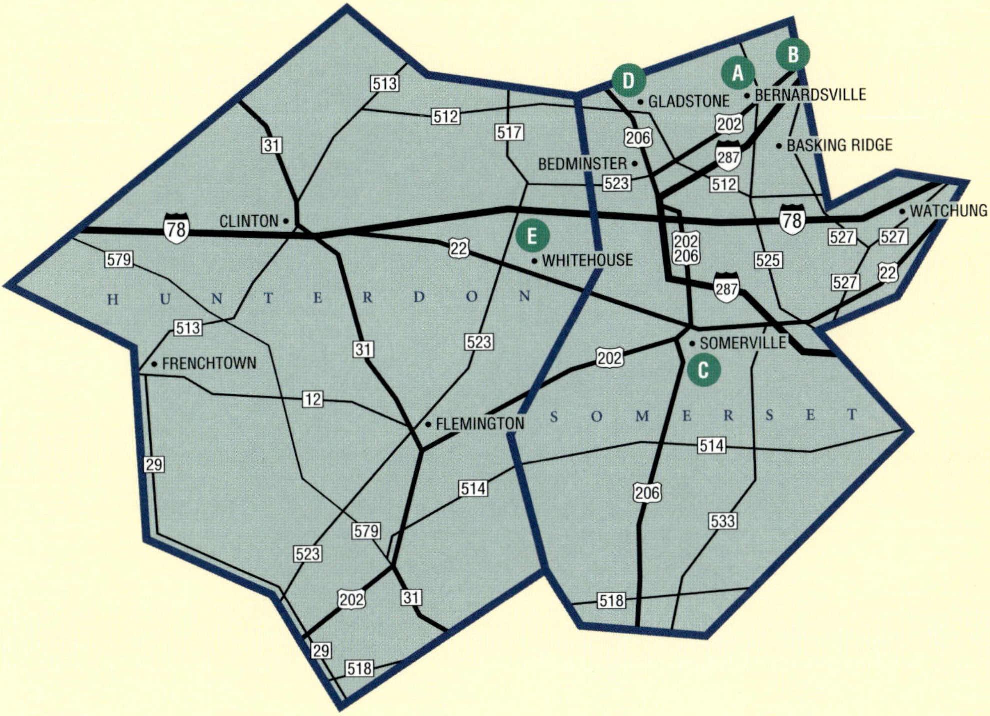

A **The Bernards Inn** ∾ *page 30*
27 Mine Brook Road • Bernardsville
Tel: 908.766.0002

B **Girafe** ∾ *page 64*
95 Morristown Road • Basking Ridge
Tel: 908.221.0017

C **La Cucina Ristorante & Cafe** ∾ *page 86*
125 West Main Street • Somerville
Tel: 908.526.4907

D **Rudolfo Ristorante** ∾ *page 114*
12 Lackawanna Avenue • Peapack-Gladstone
Tel: 908.781.1888

E **The Ryland Inn** ∾ *page 116*
Route 22 West • Whitehouse
Tel: 908.534.4011

The perfect reflection of the winemaker's art.

MUMM CUVÉE NAPA

"...the best sparkling-wine producer in California right now...particularly the rich, intense, deeply concentrated Winery Lake Cuvée. The Brut Prestige and Brut Reserve are also very well made, offering uncommon elegance and grace."

—

The Wine Spectator

STERLING VINEYARDS®

Union · Middlesex Monmouth

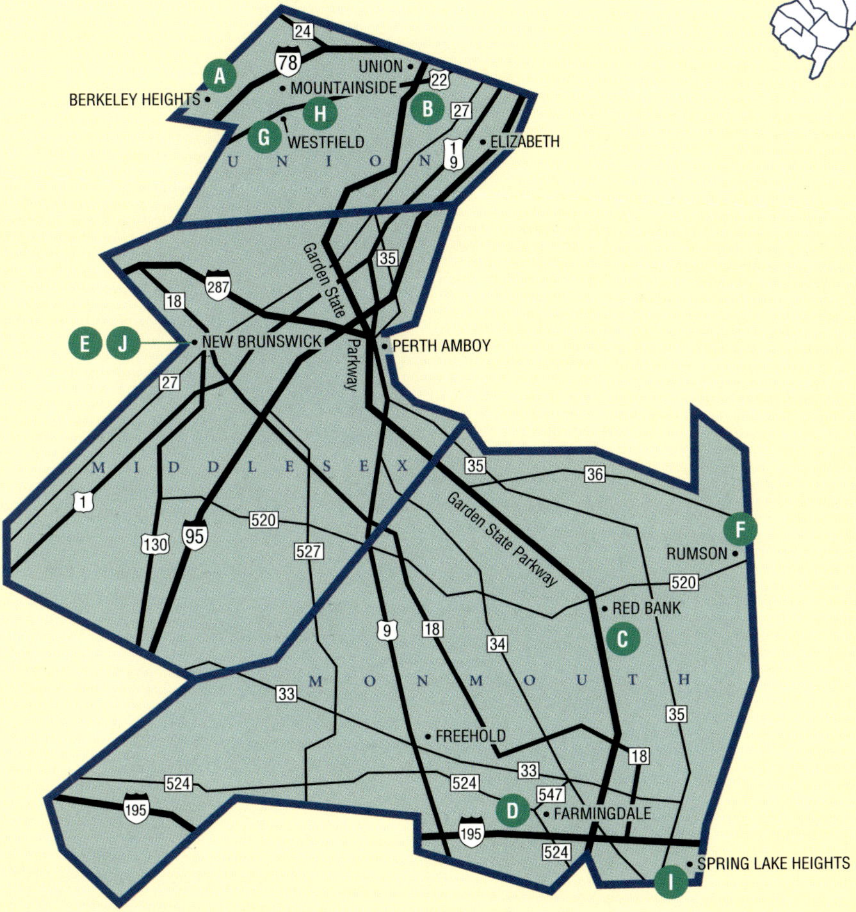

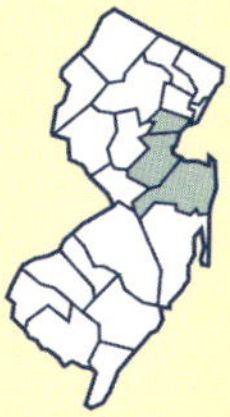

A **Auberge Swiss** ~ *page 22*
331 Springfield Avenue • Berkeley Heights
Tel: 908.665.2310

B **Benito Ristorante** ~ *page 28*
222 Galloping Hill Road • Union
Tel: 908.964.5850

C **Cucina di Roma** ~ *page 42*
6 Linden Place • Red Bank
Tel: 908.747.5121

D **The Farmingdale House** ~ *page 54*
105 Academy Street • Farmingdale
Tel: 908.938.7951

E **The Frog and The Peach** ~ *page 60*
Corner of Hiram and Dennis Streets • New Brunswick
Tel: 908.846.3216

F **Fromagerie** ~ *page 62*
26 Ridge Road • Rumson
Tel: 908.842.8088

G **Ken Marcotte** ~ *page 82*
115 Elm Street • Westfield
Tel: 908.233.2309

H **L'Affaire 22** ~ *page 88*
1099 Route 22 East • Mountainside
Tel: 908.232.4454

I **Old Mill Inn** ~ *page 106*
Old Mill Road • Spring Lake Heights
Tel: 908.449.1800

J **Panico's** ~ *page 108*
103 Church Street • New Brunswick
Tel: 908.545.6100

AUSTRALIA'S OTHER GREAT WHITE

THE SYDNEY OPERA HOUSE IS ONE OF AUSTRALIA'S GREAT WHITE LANDMARKS. THE OTHER IS JACOB'S CREEK CHARDONNAY. IT'S THE ONE WINE CRITICS ARE SINGING THE PRAISES OF.

JACOB'S CREEK®
THE LEGEND OF AUSTRALIA

ORLANDO WINES -- Sole U.S. Importer, Austin, Nichols & Co., Inc., New York, New York ©1993

MERCER · BURLINGTON

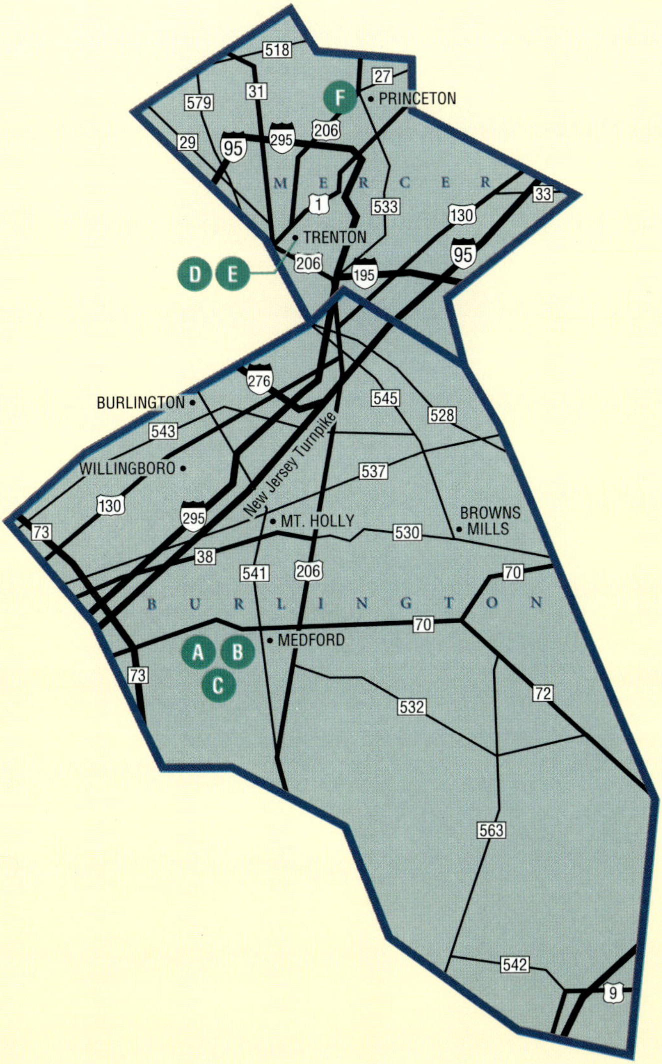

A **Beau Rivage** ~ *page 26*
128 Taunton Boulevard • Medford
Tel: 609.983.1999

B **Braddock's Tavern** ~ *page 36*
39 South Main Street • Medford
Tel: 609.654.1604

C **Chateau Silvana** ~ *page 38*
324 Main Street • Medford
Tel: 609.654.1706

D **Diamond's** ~ *page 46*
132 Kent Street • Trenton
Tel: 609.393.1000

E **La Gondola** ~ *page 90*
762 Roebling Avenue • Trenton
Tel: 609.392.0600

F **Lahiere's** ~ *page 92*
5-11 Witherspoon Street • Princeton
Tel: 609.921.2798

19

Remy Martin XO Special
Exclusively Fine Champagne Cognac

ATLANTIC · CAPE MAY

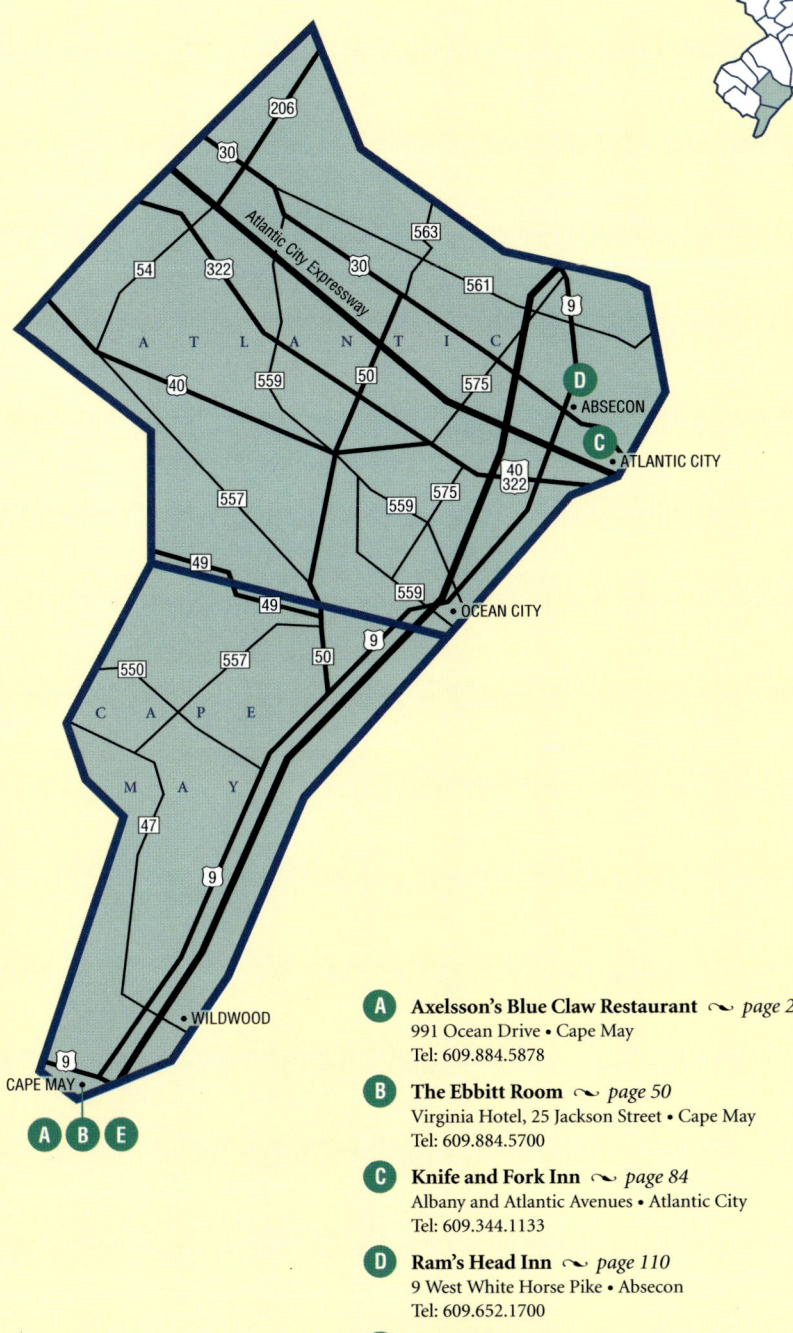

A **Axelsson's Blue Claw Restaurant** ~ *page 24*
991 Ocean Drive • Cape May
Tel: 609.884.5878

B **The Ebbitt Room** ~ *page 50*
Virginia Hotel, 25 Jackson Street • Cape May
Tel: 609.884.5700

C **Knife and Fork Inn** ~ *page 84*
Albany and Atlantic Avenues • Atlantic City
Tel: 609.344.1133

D **Ram's Head Inn** ~ *page 110*
9 West White Horse Pike • Absecon
Tel: 609.652.1700

E **Washington Inn** ~ *page 128*
801 Washington Street • Cape May
Tel: 609.884.5697

Auberge Swiss

SWISS/CONTINENTAL

Lunch Monday – Friday
Dinner Every Day

Proper Attire Please

Self-Parking

Elegant Party Facilities

Off Premise Catering

Accepts Diners Club and Other
Major Credit Cards

331 Springfield Avenue
Berkeley Heights, NJ
908.665.2310

Created by Swiss-born and trained master chef Heinz Keller, Auberge Swiss has the warmth and look of a Swiss mountain inn. A delightful taste of Switzerland is yours to experience at the Auberge Swiss restaurant. Flavorful food, nicely presented by a friendly staff, resulted in a vast clientele and earned Auberge Swiss many awards. Delicious veal, fresh fish direct from New York's Fulton Fish Market, outstanding rack of lamb and German sauerbraten are daily specialties. Authentic German Octoberfest in early October and the best game and venison menu in November and December are a few of the distinguished seasonal specialties offered throughout the year. The skillfully executed authentic Swiss cuisine is complemented by an extensive assortment of fairly priced Swiss, California, French and German wines. Little wonder Auberge Swiss has been voted one of Northern New Jersey's top four restaurants.

Veal Zurich

Ingredients

10 ounces lean milk-fed veal (from the top round)

4 tablespoons sweet butter

2 tablespoons chopped shallots

2 ounces sliced fresh mushrooms (about 3 medium)

1/3 cup dry white wine

1/3 cup brown sauce

1/3 cup heavy cream

Salt and pepper

2 teaspoons chopped fresh parsley

Spatzli, rosti potato or rice as an accompaniment

Preparation

Slice the veal against the grain into thin postage-stamp size pieces. Heat medium size skillet (10") over high heat. Add 2 tablespoons of the butter, quickly sauté veal in batches for about a minute or until brown on all sides and remove. Remove skillet from heat. Reserve veal on a warm platter.

Add rest of the butter to the skillet and melt over low heat. Raise heat to medium, add the shallots and mushrooms and sauté for 1 minute. Add the white wine and cook until the liquid is reduced to about 2 tablespoons. Add the brown sauce and juices from the browned meat in the platter. Bring to a boil, add the heavy cream and simmer the sauce until it begins to thicken. Add salt and pepper to taste. Add the meat to the skillet and simmer a minute until meat is warmed.

Place on plates and sprinkle with parsley. Serve immediately with spatzli, rosti potatoes or rice. Serves 2.

Chef's Suggested Menu

~

Viande Des Grisons
(air-dried beef from Switzerland)

Pizokel
(housemade spinach dumplings, baked with cheese and nut-flavored butter)

Lobster Delice
(chunks of lobster, scallions and sun-dried tomatoes in a light cream sauce on angel hair pasta)

Noisettes De Chevreuil "Hubertus"
(small scallops of venison, wrapped in bacon, sautéed in butter and served with shiitake mushrooms and spatzli)

Veal Zurich

Authentic Swiss Chocolate Mousse

~

Axelsson's
BLUE CLAW RESTAURANT

AMEICAN/SEAFOOD

Dinner from 5pm year-round
Country Club Casual
Self-Parking
Dinner Piano Music
Elegant Party Facilities
Accepts Diners Club and Other Major Credit Cards

991 Ocean Drive
Cape May, NJ
609.884.5878

Axelsson's Blue Claw is a handsome dining spot with luxurious European ambience that's a far cry from the typical seafood haunts that make up the seaside dining scene. ❧ Its site, adjacent to a commercial fishing fleet and marina, instills immediate confidence in the unequivocal freshness of its fish. ❧ Yet, the Blue Claw also features savory Black Angus steaks and top quality veal, poultry and seasonal game in lots of creative and classic dishes, plus many nutritious, delicious options within the American Heart Association's dietary guidelines. ❧ This unique restaurant also features splendid wines, an astute, unpretentious service staff and two fireplaces to cozy up next to during the winter months. ❧ No wonder *New Jersey Monthly* critics rated Axelsson's Blue Claw three stars, and their Reader's Choice Awards named it the "best seafood restaurant in the South".

WISCONSIN CHEDDAR AND CRAB BISQUE

INGREDIENTS

1 cup sweet butter

1 cup flour

6 cups chicken stock

1/2 cup dry white wine

1 1/4 pounds grated cheddar cheese (4 1/2 cups)

6 cups medium cream

1 tablespoon dry mustard

1 tablespoon Worcestershire sauce

1 pound jumbo lump crab meat, picked over

Salt and pepper to taste

PREPARATION

In a stock pot, melt the butter over medium heat. Stir in the flour, mix well with wire whisk and cook with frequent whisking until the mixture just begins to turn golden brown (about 2-3 minutes). Add chicken stock and wine and mix well. Bring to a boil over medium heat, whisking constantly. Simmer whisking for 10 minutes.

Reduce the heat to low and add the grated cheese, a handful at a time, until completely added. Mix frequently until cheese is all melted. Remove from the heat and strain through a fine sieve to remove any lumps. Return to low heat and add cream, mustard and Worcestershire sauce. Add crab meat, mix well and serve. Serves 12.

CHEF'S SUGGESTED MENU

∽

Wisconsin Cheddar and Crab Bisque

Smorgasbord Sampler:
A selection of smoked salmon, marinated salmon, Baltic herring, smoked trout, ceviche and raw oyster Aphrodite

Wisconsin Cheddar and Crab Soup

Black Bass en Papillote

Fresh Strawberries au Poivre

∽

Axelsson's
𝔅lue 𝔈law
Restaurant

Beau Rivage

FRENCH

Lunch Monday – Friday
Dinner Every Day

Closed Some Holidays & the
Last Two Weeks Prior to Labor Day

Gentlemen: Jackets Please

Self-Parking

Elegant Party Facilities

Accepts Diners Club and Other
Major Credit Cards

---

128 Taunton Boulevard
Medford, NJ
609.983.1999

Gerard Gehin, a master chef from Lorraine, created Beau Rivage in a wooded scene overlooking Lake Pine in the town of Medford, New Jersey. Like many of his counterparts in France, Gehin dreamed of providing fine French dining to an appreciative audience far from the hectic pace of a large city, like neighboring Philadelphia. In the 15 years since he established his country auberge, Gehin gained a loyal following of knowledgeable diners and many stars from big city restaurant critics. In 1992, Gehin's most prestigious star was added to his torque. Beau Rivage was one of only 313 restaurants in all of North America honored with the Distinguished Restaurants of North America's first annual DirōNA award that "reflects the highest standards for food, wine and spirits, service and atmosphere and value." Don't miss this classic French dining gem in the woods of Medford.

CHARLOTTE BEAU RIVAGE

Ingredients

Lady fingers

3/4 cup sugar

5 eggs separated

5 teaspoons gelatin

2 cups milk

1 cup sour cream

2 teaspoon vanilla extract

4 tablespoons Chambord liqueur

1 teaspoon raspberry extract

1 cup heavy cream, whipped

Preparation

Line a 10" spring form mold with the ladyfingers. In a bowl, beat sugar and egg yolks with a whisk until smooth and creamy. Whisk in the gelatin. Bring milk to a boil in a saucepan. Whisk about 1 cup of milk into the egg mixture and then pour all the egg mixture back into the saucepan. Cook over low heat, whisking constantly, about 15 to 20 minutes, or until the custard is thick enough to coat the back of a spoon (about 170° F). Add egg yolk mixture to the milk, whisking until very smooth. Remove from heat and add the sour cream. Separate the cream equally in 2 bowls (about 2 cups each). Add vanilla extract to one, and Chambord and raspberry extract to the other bowl. Chill mixture until it is the consistency of raw egg whites. Whip egg whites until they just hold stiff peaks and fold equally into each bowl. Fold equal portions of whipped cream into each bowl. Pour the vanilla mixture into the spring form lined with lady fingers. Pour the Chambord mixture over the vanilla mixture (forming 2 layers). Refrigerate until firm.

To serve, slice a wedge of the Charlotte and place it on a cold plate. Surround the slice with melba sauce. Garnish the top with a dollop of whipped cream decorated with a fresh raspberry and a mint leaf.

Chef's Suggested Menu

~

Le Fond d'Artichaut Farci Strasbourg
(artichoke hearts, stuffed
with foie gras and mushrooms,
served gratinee)

La Crevette "Sweet Water" Grillee
(grilled fresh water prawns
with a spicy lemon garlic sauce,
crab meat and dill)

Le Ris de Veau Sauté
(sautéed veal sweetbreads with
wild mushrooms and thyme)

L'Entrecote de Boeuf "Pine Barrens"
(sirloin steak with
a unique cranberry, truffle and
peppercorn sauce)

Charlotte Beau Rivage, Sauce Melba

~

BEAU RIVAGE

We Welcome

BENITO RISTORANTE

ITALIAN

Dinner Monday – Saturday
Lunch Monday – Friday

*Jackets Required
for Gentlemen in Evenings*

Valet Parking on Weekends

*Private Party Facilities
for Weddings,
Rehearsal Dinners, Social Parties
& Corporate Events*

*Accepts Diners Club and Other
Major Credit Cards*

---

222 GALLOPING HILL ROAD
UNION, NJ
908.964.5850

BENITO RISTORANTE IS ACCLAIMED FOR ITS SPLENDID READINGS OF THE SUBTLE CUISINE OF ITALY'S NORTHERN PROVINCES, COUPLED WITH ITS SOPHISTICATED SELECTION OF ADMIRABLE WINES, A MASTERFUL WAIT STAFF AND SUPERIOR SURROUNDINGS. ❧ HOWEVER, THE OWNER WHO LAUNCHED HIS CELEBRATED NAMESAKE RESTAURANT, BENITO HISENAJ, IS ITS PREMIER ASSET. ❧ THIS CONSUMMATE PIEDMONT RESTAURATEUR FROM TURIN GUIDES DINERS ON A GASTRONOMIC EXCURSION OF HIS HOMELAND — HIS EXPERT CHEFS PLEASING PALATES WITH THEIR DISTINCTIVE DISHES. ❧ SOME TRUE TASTES OF THIS STRAIGHTFORWARD TANTALIZING GOURMET COOKERY INCLUDE GRILLED WHOLE SHRIMP DRIZZLED WITH EXTRA VIRGIN OLIVE OIL, POACHED FRESH FISH WITH A DELICATELY PIQUANT AGRODOLCE SAUCE, A SIMPLE ROASTED CHICKEN DUSTED WITH FRESH ROSEMARY AND A COLOSSAL, SNOWY BROILED VEAL CHOP UNDER A MANTLE OF MULTICOLORED PEPPERS. ❧ THOSE WHO SAVE SOME ROOM FOR DESSERT ARE REWARDED WITH A CLOUD–LIKE AUTHENTIC ITALIAN CHEESECAKE THAT'S SECOND TO NONE.

RAVIOLI PIEMONTESE

INGREDIENTS

- 1 tablespoon butter
- 2 tablespoons olive oil
- 1/2 cup onion, diced
- 1 tablespoon garlic, diced
- 1 spring rosemary, diced (about 1 teaspoon)
- 1/2 pound of lean beef, cut into 1" cubes
- Salt and pepper to taste
- 2 tablespoons flour
- 1/2 cup beef stock
- 3 canned, peeled San Marzano tomatoes, drained, pureéd (about 1 cup)
- 1/2 cup blanched, drained, squeezed dry and finely chopped spinach
- 1/4 cup freshly grated parmesan cheese
- 1 egg beaten
- 1 pound of prepared food processor pasta dough, rolled and made into ravioli (see Gourmet Pantry)

PREPARATION

Make the meat for the filling and the sauce: In a skillet melt the butter in the oil over medium heat. Add the onion, the garlic and the rosemary and sauté for 3 minutes (or until soft). Add the beef and brown on all sides (about 3 minutes). Sprinkle with the salt, the pepper and the flour and add the stock and the tomatoes. Bring to a boil. cover, lower heat and simmer until tender (about 1 hour).

Make the filling: Remove the meat from the sauce in which it was cooked with a slotted spoon and allow it to cool to room temperature. Put the meat through a meat grinder twice. Add the spinach, the parmesan cheese and the eggs to the ground meat mixture and mix well to incorporate.

Make the sauce: Put the sauce through a fine sieve, return to a sauce pan and let simmer, covered.

Make the ravioli: Prepare the ravioli by the Gourmet Pantry Section procedures for "Food Processor Pasta Dough", "To Roll the Pasta Dough" and "To Make Ravioli".

In a kettle of boiling salted water, cook the ravioli in 2 batches for 4 minutes, or until they are al dente, transferring them as they are cooked with a slotted spoon to buttered jelly-roll pans, and keep them warm, covered, in a preheated 200° F oven. Arrange ravioli on warm plates, coat with the sauce and serve with freshly ground pepper and parmesan cheese to taste.

CHEF'S SUGGESTED MENU

Spiedino Valdostano
(fried brochette of Fontina cheese and ham)

Insalata Cesare
(Caesar salad)

Linguine alla Benito
(imported al dente linguine tossed with anchovies, thinly sliced red peppers, garlic and a delicate tomato sauce)

Cernia Bollito Agrodolce
(poached red snapper with a savory lemon-scented extra virgin olive oil blend)

Medaglioni de Filetto di Bue Maison
(mignonettes of beef with pate and madiera sauce)

Torta di Formaggio
(ethereal Italian cheesecake)

The Bernards Inn

American / Contemporary

Lunch & Dinner
Monday – Saturday

Jackets Required for Dinner

Self-Parking

Luxurious Overnight
Accommodations
Hotel Open 24 Hours
21 Guest Rooms

Customized Menus &
Catering Facilities

Accepts Diners Club and Other
Major Credit Cards

---

27 Mine Brook Road
Bernardsville, NJ
908.766.0002

The Bernards Inn is an elegant turn-of-the-century restaurant and hotel nestled in Somerset Hills, the heart of Bernardsville. ❧ Under the direction of partners Alice Rochat and Chef Edward Stone, the restaurant features progressive contemporary American cuisine prepared with classic French fundamentals. ❧ The sautéed foie gras bursts with flavor and the delicately prepared medallions of veal with morel mushrooms and angel hair pasta are exceptional. ❧ The Bernards Inn wine list is diversified and offers superb selections to complement Chef Stone's masterful presentations. ❧ The Bernards Inn restaurant and lounge, meeting and banquet rooms, as well as the newly renovated and magnificent ballroom, play host to business and social occasions of every kind.

Wild Mushroom Soup

Ingredients

- 1/4 cup olive oil
- 4 tablespoons unsalted butter
- 4 medium Spanish onions, thinly sliced, about 10 cups
- 1 pound wild mushrooms, coarsely chopped (any combination of oyster mushrooms, chanterelles or shiitake)
- 8 to 10 garlic cloves, peeled and crushed
- 1 bunch fresh thyme, coarsely chopped
- 1 cup all-purpose flour
- 2 cups dry white wine
- 4 cups chicken stock or broth
- 1 cup heavy cream
- Kosher salt and fresh milled pepper

Preparation

Add oil and butter to a heavy gauge stock pot over high heat. Heat until butter is melted and the oil is quite hot. Add the onions and cook over low heat, stirring frequently about 15 to 20 minutes or until the onions are golden brown. Add the mushrooms, garlic and thyme and cook the mixture, stirring occasionally for 10 minutes.

Add the flour and cook the mixture, stirring, for 5 minutes. Whisk in the wine and the chicken stock and bring to a boil, whisking. Simmer the soup for 15 minutes, add the cream and bring the soup to a boil. Add the salt and pepper to taste.

Remove the soup from the heat. Pureé the soup in a food processor (or blender) until smooth. Pass the soup, in small batches, through a fine hole strainer. Adjust the seasonings. Heat before serving, adding water or additional chicken stock to thin the soup if desired. Serves 8-10 one cup servings.

Chef's Suggested Menu

~

Ballotine of Salmon with a Two Caviar and Dill Vin Blanc

Wild Mushroom Soup

Sautéed Sweetbreads with Sherry Wine and Caramelized Onions

Roast Pheasant with a Sun-dried Cherry and Armagnac Au Jus

Wild Rice, Baby Squash and Cranberry Compo

Hazelnut Creme Brulee

~

BLACK FOREST INN

GERMAN/CONTINENTAL

Lunch Monday, Wednesday – Friday
Dinner Wednesday – Monday
Closed Tuesdays

Proper Dress Please

Self-Parking

Friday Night Piano Music

Elegant Wedding & Party Facilities

Gourmet Dinners on Request

Accepts Diners Club and Other
Major Credit Cards

249 ROUTE 206
STANHOPE, NJ
201.347.3344

Heinz Aichem, who originated the Black Forest Inn in 1978, is a world-class chef with extensive culinary experience at the finest restaurants in Switzerland, France and England. When he conceived of the Black Forest Inn, Aichem's dream of introducing Americans to authentic German haute cuisine — like the food served in Germany's posh dining spots — became a reality. In the last 14 years Heinz Aichem and the Black Forest Inn have received numerous honors from *The New York Times*, *New Jersey Monthly*, gourmet societies and tributes from Bob Lape, as well as other reviewers too numerous to mention. The strikingly handsome restaurant, which resembles a deluxe German country inn, has an extensive wine cellar, proficient unpretentious service and sumptuous cuisine rarely seen this side of the Atlantic.

Seafood Quenelles in Champagne Sauce

Ingredients

1/2 pound shrimp, peeled and deveined
1/2 pound salmon fillet
1/2 pound turbot fillet (flounder optional)
4 egg whites
1 pint heavy cream
Salt and white pepper
3 quarts fish stock
2 cups dry white wine
1 tablespoon salt
1 bay leaf
Bouquet garni

Champagne sauce:
3 cloves shallots, diced (about 1/4 pound)
1 clove garlic, diced
2 sprigs fresh thyme, minced
2 tablespoons butter
2 cups dry white wine
2 cups fish stock
3 cups heavy cream
2 tablespoons creme fraiche
1 tablespoon corn starch (if necessary)
1/2 cup Noilly Prat (dry vermouth)
1 cup champagne
2 tablespoons fresh chives, snipped
Juice of one lemon (about 3 tablespoons)

Preparation

Place shrimp, salmon and turbot in the bowl of a food processor with egg whites and run at high speed until thick. Slowly add cream and continue to mix until a very smooth consistency is achieved. Season with salt and pepper to taste. Bring fish stock to a boil and add white wine, salt, bay leaf and bouquet garni. When the liquid returns to a boil, take 2 large kitchen spoons (wet with water) with a half-spoonful of the mixture (about 1 tablespoon) in one. Form a quenelle by rolling the mixture off one spoon to the other. Drop into the boiling liquid and continue with the rest of the mixture. Let quenelles come to a boil once more and remove from heat (about 1 to 2 minutes).

Sauté shallots, garlic and thyme in butter over low heat until they are transparent. Deglaze pan with the wine and reduce by boiling to a 1/2 cup. Add fish stock and reduce by half. Add cream and creme fraiche and bring to a boil. If not thick, thicken by mixing corn starch with an equal amount of cold water (in separate container) and add slowly to the boiling cream to achieve a cream soup consistency (about 2 cups). In a separate sauce pan add the vermouth and champagne and reduce by boiling to a 1/2 cup. Add this liquid to the stock. Strain through a fine sieve into a clean sauce pan. Add chives and salt and pepper to taste and lemon juice to finish. Can be served over rice or julienne vegetables. Serves 4 to 6, about 25 quenelles.

Chef's Suggested Menu

Potato Leek Soup

Fresh Seafood Quenelles in Champagne Sauce

Pan Roasted Duck Breast with Apple Cassis

Roasted Filet of Veal with Wild Mushroom Sauce

Hazelnut Mousse on a Fresh Raspberry Coulis

Black Forest Inn

We Welcome

BLACK HORSE INN

AMERICAN/CONTINENTAL

Dinner Tuesday – Sunday
Country Club Casual
Valet Parking
Piano Music Every Night
Elegant Facilities for Private Parties

Black Horse Pub:
Open for Lunch & Dinner Every Day
Sunday Brunch

Entertainment Fridays & Saturdays

Accepts Diners Club and Other
Major Credit Cards

ONE WEST MAIN STREET
MENDHAM, NJ
201.543.7300

A STAGECOACH STOP DATING BACK TO 1742, THE BLACK HORSE INN HAS BEEN UNDER THE MANAGEMENT OF THE KNAPP FAMILY FOR THE PAST 25 YEARS. LIVING UP TO ITS CREDO – "ONLY THE BEST FOR OUR CUSTOMERS" – MAKES THIS DINING TRADITION VERY POPULAR WITH THE HORSEY-SET AND CORPORATE TYPES ALIKE. WHEN YOU HAVE A CRAVING FOR TRULY THE FINEST PRIME RIBS, DRY-AGED SIRLOIN STEAK, FRESH JUMBO LUMP CRABMEAT, FIELD GREEN SALADS, GRILLED FRESH TUNA OR LOBSTERS THAT TASTE LIKE THEY WERE JUST PLUCKED FROM THE SEA, THE BLACK HORSE INN IS THE PLACE FOR YOU. IF YOUR TASTE BUDS ARE IN NEED OF A THIN-CRUST DESIGNER PIZZA, CHARBROILED BURGERS, STEAMED CLAMS, OYSTERS ON THE HALF SHELL OR BABY BACK RIBS, SET YOUR SIGHTS FOR THE BLACK HORSE PUB.

ROASTED TOMATO AND GRILLED SCALLOPS OVER MESCLUN SALAD

INGREDIENTS

- 3 large tomatoes
- 4 tablespoons extra virgin olive oil
- 2 tablespoons fresh thyme (or 4 tablespoons dried)
- Salt and freshly ground pepper to taste
- 2 tablespoons fresh orange juice
- 1 1/2 tablespoons finely minced shallots (yellow onions optional)
- 1/2 teaspoon grated orange peel
- 1/2 teaspoon grated lemon peel
- 1/2 teaspoon finely minced fresh ginger
- 1 pound sea scallops, (about 12)
- 4 cups loosely packed mixed baby greens (mesclun salad mix)

PREPARATION

Core tops from tomatoes. Place into 5 quarts of boiling water for 30 seconds, remove and place in a large pot of ice water for 1 minute. Remove and drain tomatoes. Peel, cut in half side-to-side and remove seeds. Chop one of the tomatoes coarsely. Place the other tomatoes, cut side down, on a sheet pan. In a small bowl, mix 2 tablespoons of the olive oil with thyme, salt and pepper to taste. Brush tomatoes all over with oil mixture and bake in preheated oven at 300° F for 20 minutes. Cool roasted tomatoes to room temperature. Cut into strips and reserve.

In a blender, combine the rest of the olive oil, orange juice, minced shallots, orange peel, lemon peel and fresh ginger with chopped tomato and juice from roasted tomatoes. Blend well to make a dressing. Add salt and pepper to taste.

Grill the scallops on a lightly oiled grill, turning them for about 4 to 5 minutes, or until they are just cooked through. Sprinkle with salt and pepper to taste.

Place equal parts of the mesclun salad on 4 dinner-size plates. Top salads with equal parts of grilled scallops and roasted tomatoes. Stir dressing well and drizzle over the salads. Serve immediately. Serves 4.

CHEF'S SUGGESTED MENU

Lobster Bisque

Roasted Tomato and Grilled Scallops over Mesclun Salad

Grilled Tuna, Jalapeno Honey Tartar Sauce

Prime Ribs of Beef, Baked Stuffed Potato, Asparagus with Hollandaise

Chocolate Mousse Pie

Braddock's Tavern

AMERICAN/CONTEMPORARY

Lunch Monday – Friday
Sunday Brunch
Dinner Daily

Proper Attire

Self-Parking in a Private Lot

Private Party Accommodations

Accepts Diners Club and Other Major Credit Cards

39 South Main Street
Medford, NJ
609.654.1604

Built in 1843, Braddock's Tavern is steeped in colonial tradition and nestled in the charm of the historic Medford Village. Today, it is well known for its expertly prepared, award-winning cuisine, impeccable service and romantic candlelight dining in a beautifully preserved colonial inn. All these attributes have earned it numerous accolades which include: "The Best of the Best, Five Star Dining Award, Top 5 American Traditional Restaurants in the Nation," and the "Best of the Best" in *New Jersey Monthly* Readers' Choice Awards. These all highlight a fine tradition of quality and are treasured by owners Joe and Linda Mondelli, General Manager Rob Mondelli and Executive Chef Joel Gaughan. This highly acclaimed establishment harmonizes splendid cuisine, world-class wines and admirable service with an ambiance that draws character from the building's authentic colonial roots.

Lobster Terrine

Ingredients

Vanilla Vinaigrette:
1 vanilla bean
1 tablespoon of sugar dissolved in 1/2 cup cold water
1/2 cup safflower oil
1/2 cup rice vinegar

Lobster Terrine:
2 8 ounce lobster tails, removed from the shell
Juice of 1 lemon (about 1/4 cup)
1 cup dry white wine
9 large romaine lettuce leaves (about one head)
3 tablespoons sweet butter
1 cup leeks, white part only, washed and diced
1 cup carrots, diced
1 cup fresh peas
1 pound sea scallops, quartered
1 egg
1 cup heavy cream

Preparation

Vinaigrette: Split the vanilla bean lengthwise and remove seeds. Add the seeds to a bowl with the rest of the ingredients. Allow to macerate for 2 hours or overnight. Whisk to emulsify just prior to using.

Lobster Terrine: In a large glass bowl, combine the lobster meat with the lemon juice and wine and marinate for 2 hours in a refrigerator. Blanch the lettuce leaves in simmering water (3 to 4 minutes), remove, cool and blot dry. In a skillet melt butter (moderate heat), add the leeks, the carrots and the peas and sauté until leeks are soft (about 3 to 5 minutes). Remove and reserve. In a food processor, combine the scallops and egg and pureé until smooth. Add the cream and process until well incorporated. Place in a bowl and fold in the sautéed vegetables.

Butter an 8 inch by 4 inch terrine. Line the bottom with a lettuce leaf. Line the sides of the pan with remaining leaves, making sure they overhang all sides of the terrine by about 3 inches. Place 1 inch of the scallop pureé on the bottom of the pan. Dry the lobster and place on top of the scallop pureé. Top with the remaining scallop pureé and cover with the lettuce. Cover the terrine with buttered aluminum foil, place in a simmering water bath in a preheated oven (350°F) for 1 hour. Remove, cool to room temperature and refrigerate overnight. Cut in 1/2" thick slices and serve on a chilled plate surrounded by the vanilla vinaigrette. Serves 4.

Chef's Suggested Menu

Grilled Aubergine
(layers of eggplant, smoked mozzarella, sweet onion marmalade, black forest ham, tomatoes and sliced shiitake mushrooms)

Lobster Terrine

Filet Jonathan
(grilled filet mignon, topped with an herbal crust and placed on a pond of reduced red wine sauce)

Potatoes au Gratin, Buttered Snap Peas and Glazed Baby Carrots with a Vanilla Sauce

Chocolate Pâté with Raspberry Sauce

Braddock's Tavern

CHATEAU SILVANA

ITALIAN

Lunch Monday – Friday
Dinner Daily
Champagne Brunch Sunday

Jackets Suggested

Self-Parking

Wedding & Private Party Facilities

Accepts Diners Club and Other Major Credit Cards

324 Main Street
Medford, NJ
609.654.1706

Situated in a handsomely restored 18th century historic home surrounded by farmland, Chateau Silvana has a clear claim to uniqueness. Like the celebrated trattorie in the Tuscan countryside, this charming restaurant features distinguished Northern Italian food based on premier raw materials and the consummate cooking skills of proprietor-chef Tony Bonfiglio. The glorious fare is masterfully served in a cozy atmosphere teamed with a sophisticated set of wines. Little wonder Chateau Silvana is consistently praised by patrons and critics alike, and received the "Best of the Best" honor in the *New Jersey Monthly* Readers' Choice Awards. A sampling of Chateau Silvana's glorious dishes include adventurous ravioli stuffed with lobster and bathed in an opulent pink cream sauce spiked with vodka plus an intensely flavorful veal chop stuffed with imported fontina and sun-dried tomatoes and placed on a savory port wine sauce.

Broeto — Venetian Fish Soup

Ingredients

- 8 cups fish stock
- 1/2 lemon
- 3 large ripe tomatoes, peeled and chopped (3 cups)
- Salt to taste
- 1/2 cup olive oil
- 3 cloves garlic, finely chopped (3 tablespoons)
- 1 onion, finely chopped (2/3 cup)
- 3 tablespoons chopped parsley (2-3 sprigs)
- 1 1/2 pounds North Atlantic sole (cut into 2" pieces)
- 1 pound orange roughy fillet (cut into 2" pieces)
- 1 1/2 pounds fillet of Norwegian salmon (cut into 2" pieces)
- 12 slices Italian bread, deep fried crisp and drained
- Grated parmesan cheese to taste (1/2 cup)

Preparation

In a soup pot, add the fish stock, the lemon, the tomatoes and the salt to taste and cook over moderate heat for 25 minutes. Reduce heat and simmer the soup while preparing the fish.

In a large skillet, add the oil and sauté the garlic, the onion and the parsley over moderate heat until golden. Add the fish (sole first, roughy second and then the salmon) and sauté on both sides, in batches, until just cooked through (about 2-3 minutes each side). Add the fish to the soup and simmer for 2 minutes. Place 2 slices of the fried bread in each of the separate soup bowls. Carefully add the soup to the bowls. Top with parmesan cheese and serve. Serves 6.

Chef's Suggested Menu

"Broeto" Veneziana
(A classic Venetian fish soup)

Giardiniera Alpina
(blanched medley of asparagus, broccoli, sun-dried tomatoes and mushrooms)

Ravioli Lombardese
(ravioli filled with a veal forcemeat in a spinach accented cream sauce, artichoke garnish)

Fagiano e Quaglie Arborale
(roasted pheasant and quail with apricot brandy demi glaze)

Pesche alla Piemontese
(peaches stuffed with an almond macaroon accented peach pureé)

We Welcome

CREATIONS
RESTAURANT & MEETING PLACE

AMERICAN/CONTEMPORARY

Lunch Monday – Friday
Dinner Tuesday – Sunday

Country Club Casual

Self-Parking

Nightly Entertainment Featuring
Live Music in the Dining Room
and the Cocktail Lounge

Available for Private Functions
during Non-Operating Hours

Accepts Diners Club and Other
Major Credit Cards

54 MAIN STREET
MADISON, NJ
201.966.0252

CREATIONS RESTAURANT & MEETING PLACE IS A CONVIVIAL GATHERING PLACE FOR AN EXCEEDINGLY COSMOPOLITAN CROWD AND AN ATTRACTIVE SHOWPLACE FOR THE BRILLIANTLY CREATIVE DISHES OF CHEF DE CUISINE/PROPRIETOR TIMOTHY SCHAFER. SCHAFER'S ADVENTUROUS CUISINE — SOLIDLY BASED ON CLASSIC COOKING TECHNIQUES COUPLED WITH A LIBERAL DASH OF FRENCH, ITALIAN, ORIENTAL, CAJUN AND SOUTHWESTERN ACCENTS — CONSISTENTLY CAPTIVATES CRITICS AND PATRONS ALIKE. THESE INNOVATIVE CREATIONS, WHICH NEVER OVERSHADOW THE INHERENT TASTE OF THE CHOICE NATURAL INGREDIENTS, ARE AT THE FOREFRONT OF CONTEMPORARY AMERICAN CUISINE. DESSERTS ARE A DREAM, THE WINE SELECTION IS THOUGHTFULLY MATCHED TO THE FOOD AND THE ATTENTIVE SERVICE STAFF BLENDS WITH THE EASY ATMOSPHERE OF THIS EXCITING RESTAURANT WHERE THERE ARE NO DREARY DISHES.

Pan Seared Tuna Steak
in a Sesame Crust with Oriental Vegetables and a Spicy Thai Chili Salsa

Ingredients

For the salsa:
- 20 Thai chilies, (or 6 diced green jalapenos)
- 6 garlic cloves
- 1 bunch scallions, sliced on the bias (1 cup)
- 1/3 cup vegetable oil
- 1 tablespoons sesame oil

For the tuna:
- 3 tablespoons sesame seeds
- 2 bunches cilantro, washed, squeezed dry and chopped (1/2 cups)
- 1/2 cups ground fresh bread crumbs
- 4 tablespoons vegetable oil
- 4 6 oz. yellowfin tuna steaks

For the vegetables:
- 1 large onion (1/2 pound)
- 1/2 cup bamboo shoots
- 1/2 cup water chestnuts
- 12 shiitake mushrooms, stems removed
- 1 teaspoon fresh ginger, peeled
- 1/2 red pepper
- 1/2 green pepper
- 1/2 yellow pepper
- 1 bunch scallions, sliced on the bias (1 cup)
- 2 tablespoons vegetable oil
- 1 teaspoon sesame oil
- 16 canned baby corn, drained and cut lengthwise
- 1/4 cup sake (or dry white wine)
- 1/4 cup chicken stock
- 1 tablespoon soy sauce
- 1 tablespoon sweet butter
- A dash each of salt, pepper, worcestershire sauce and Tabasco sauce

Preparation

Make the salsa: Thinly slice vegetables, heat the oil and toss with the vegetables. Allow to seep for 5 minutes minimum.

Make the tuna: Combine sesame seeds with cilantro and bread crumbs. Pat the crumb mixture on both surfaces of the tuna. Heat oil in a skillet over high heat. Just before oil begins to smoke, add the tuna and sear both sides for about 1-2 minutes (done in 2 batches with 2 tablespoons of vegetable oil per batch). Place fried tuna in a baking pan and bake in a 350° F preheated oven for 5 to 7 minutes.

Make oriental vegetables: Thinly slice onions, bamboo shoots, water chestnuts, mushrooms and ginger. Cut peppers into 1" x 1" pieces and scallions into 1" long pieces. Heat oil in a skillet over high heat. Just before it begins to smoke add the onions, peppers and scallions first and sauté with constant stirring for 1 minute. Add mushrooms and stir fry 1 minute longer. Add together corns, bamboo shoots, water chestnuts and ginger. Stir and cook for 1 minute longer. Add the sake, chicken stock and soy sauce and boil over high heat to reduce liquids slightly. Add butter and seasoning and mix well to finish and remove from heat.

Assemble: Place vegetables on a large platter. Place tuna on top of the vegetables. Garnish with small portions of salsa around the perimeter of the vegetables. You may also garnish with strips of deep fried wonton skins, sliced chives and carrot flowers. Serves 4.

Chef's Suggested Menu

Lobster
and Lemongrass Consomme
with Smoked Shrimp Wontons

Grilled Beef Satay
with Sweet and Sour
Peanut Sauce

Pan Seared Tuna Steak
in a Sesame Crust
with Oriental Vegetables and a
Spicy Thai Chili Salsa

Flourless Chocolate Ginger Torte
with Roasted Banana Sauce
and Coconut Ice Cream

We Welcome

Cucina di Roma

ITALIAN

Lunch Tuesday – Friday
Dinner Tuesday – Sunday
Closed Monday

Dress: Casually Elegant

Self-Parking Lot
Adjacent to Restaurant

Party Facilities

Accepts Diners Club and Other
Major Credit Cards

6 Linden Place
Red Bank, NJ
908.747.5121

Created by seasoned professional restaurateurs Woody Futrelle and Giesela Smith and their partner, Master Chef Michael Woodburry, Cucina di Roma rocketed to stardom. Specifically, in the years since its inception, this stellar restaurant was applauded by the critics of The New York Times, The Star Ledger and New Jersey Monthly, and accorded top grades in the Zagat Tri-State Restaurant Survey (published in 1993). Cucina di Roma's faithful renditions of classic and modern Roman cuisine are paired with epicurean delights from Italy's northern provinces. True to the essence of haute Italian cuisine, Cucina de Roma's captivating creations are based on the prudent use of herbs and sauces to accentuate the natural tastes of respectfully prepared, prime ingredients. These attractively presented standout dishes are complemented by an extensive selection of splendid, top-value wines, a masterful service staff and notably handsome, cosmopolitan surroundings.

RED BANK VEAL CHOP CALABRESE

INGREDIENTS

2 rib veal chops cut 2" thick

8 tablespoons olive oil

Salt and pepper to taste

2 teaspoons fresh thyme, chopped

1 medium red bell pepper, cut into 1" slices vertically, ribs and seeds removed

4 cloves garlic, diced

1/4 cup dry Marsala wine

2 tablespoons red wine vinegar

2 tablespoons fresh lemon juice (about 1 lemon)

1 cup white veal stock

PREPARATION

Season the veal chops with 2 tablespoons of the olive oil, the salt, the pepper and 1 teaspoon of the thyme. Set aside at room temperature for 10 to 15 minutes.

In a heavy gauge sauté pan over high heat add the remaining olive oil. Sauté the red pepper slices until lightly browned on the edges (about 3 minutes). Add the garlic and sauté until lightly golden. Add the Marsala wine and bring to a boil. Reduce the volume by 1/4 (about 3 minutes). Add the vinegar and the lemon juice and bring to a boil. Reduce the volume by one half (about 5 minutes). Add the stock and bring to a boil. Reduce the liquid until syrupy (the consistency of maple syrup). Add the remaining thyme and salt and pepper to taste. Keep warm over low heat.

Grill the veal chop in a preheated broiler over moderately high heat until cooked to the desired degree (about 6 minutes per side for medium). Divide the sauce equally and pour onto 2 warm plates. Place one chop on each of the plates with wild rice.

CHEF'S SUGGESTED MENU

**Seafood Sausage with
a Lemon-Fresh Herb Cream Sauce**

**Cream of Tomato Soup
with Fresh Dill**

**Arugula Salad, Tomato, Fresh Basil
with Herb Vinaigrette**

**Veal Chop Calabrese
on a Piquant Sauce of Fresh
Peppers and Garlic**

**Fresh Fruit,
Grand Marnier Zabaglione**

Cucina di Roma

DENNIS FOY'S TOWNSQUARE

AMERICAN / CONTEMPORARY

Lunch Monday – Friday
Dinner Every Day

Jackets Required

Self-Parking

Elegant Corporate & Party Facilities

Accepts Diners Club and Other
Major Credit Cards

6 ROOSEVELT AVENUE
CHATHAM, NJ
201.701.0303

Dennis Foy, who is regarded as one of America's premier chefs, established his reputation in New Jersey at the Tarragon Tree in Chatham. After gaining national acclaim as the originator and executive chef of Manhattan's celebrated Mondrian restaurant in the '80's, Mr. Foy returned to Chatham to establish Dennis Foy's Townsquare. In this attractive, unpretentious setting, Chef Foy presents culinary creations on the cutting edge of American cuisine coupled with a splendid selection of wines and admirable service. The dramatic, eye-appealing dishes reflect the wholesome cookery of America in the '90's. Examples of Chef Foy's gastronomic treats, which change with the availability of super-fresh ingredients, include a spring pea soup with smoked salmon, black pepper and chive, or seared salmon with red wine and spring leeks. Desserts are also a dream at this "world-class" restaurant.

Roasted Venison, Spaghetti Squash, Cranberries

Ingredients

- 1 16-20 ounce venison loin (from the leg optional)
- 1/2 pound caul fat
- 1 tablespoon tarragon oil (or one sprig tarragon heated for 2 minutes in vegetable oil and strained)
- 1/2 cup mirepoix brunoise (3 tablespoons of small dice of carrots, celery and onion)
- 1 sprig each of tarragon, thyme and sage
- 2 tablespoons butter
- 1/2 cup vegetable stock
- 1/2 cup venison stock (or beef)
- 1 2-3 pound spaghetti squash
- 3 ounces purple cabbage (1 cup)
- 1/4 pound bacon (or foie fat)
- Salt and pepper
- 4 brussel sprouts
- 1 ounce fresh cranberries or currants

Preparation

Remove the loin from the saddle, season well and wrap in caul fat. Tie the loin every 1/4 ".

In a sauté pan, bring the tarragon oil to temperature and lightly sauté the mirepoix (about 2 minutes). Remove and set aside. In the same pan, place the loin and brown it on all sides. Place in a baking pan with the mirepoix brunoise, herbs and butter. Roast in a preheated 350° F oven for 20 minutes (rare to medium rare). Set aside to rest. Pour off excess oil and butter (about 1/4 cup) and deglaze the pan with a vegetable stock. Add venison stock and boil to reduce by half. Strain, season to taste and set aside.

Boil spaghetti squash in water to cover for 35 to 45 minutes, turning occasionally on all sides. Remove and rest. When it is cool, slice open, remove seeds, separate strands and discard shell. Sauté strands in one tablespoon butter over medium heat. Season to taste and set aside.

Slice the purple cabbage thinly and blanch quickly in salted boiling water (1 1/2 minutes). Drain well. To finish, sweat bacon (or foie fat) in a sauté pan. Remove bacon, add blanched cabbage and sauté until tender (1 to 2 minutes). Season with salt and pepper. Set aside and keep warm.

Blanch brussel sprouts until tender in boiling salted water. Remove and drain well. Peel outer leaves so that what remains are bulbs of even size. Sauté gently to heat thoroughly and season with salt and pepper.

To serve, slice the venison to achieve 6 even medallions. Fill a small fan mold with 1/2 of the spaghetti squash and 1/2 the purple cabbage. Unmold onto the center of a large plate, top with 1/2 the sautéed brussel sprouts. Repeat this process for a second plate. Around the rim of the molded vegetables, arrange the venison and scatter the cranberries or currants and sauce. Serves 2.

Chef's Suggested Menu

Tuna and Salmon Tartar, Wasabi Oil

Black Risotto, Grilled Shrimp

Sautéed Black Sea Bass, Herb Broth

Roasted Pigeon, Portobello and Foie Napoleon, Peppered Cabbage

Sautéed Loin of Veal, Root Flours, Fava Beans Mariniere

Chocolate Souffle

We Welcome

Diamond's

ITALIAN

Lunch Monday – Friday
Dinner Daily to Midnight
Cocktail Lounge Open to 2 AM

Proper Attire Please

Self-Parking in Convenient
Parking Lots

Elegant Facilities for
Lunches, Dinners, Banquets
& Business Functions

Accepts Diners Club and Other
Major Credit Cards

---

132 Kent Street
Trenton, NJ
609.393.1000

Ten years ago, brothers Anthony and Thomas Zucchetti transformed a "shot and a beer" neighborhood saloon on the block where they were born into a fine dining gem called Diamond's. In the historic Chambersburg restaurant district of Trenton, this handsomely refurbished ristorante soon became the setting for a sophisticated blend of Continental and Italian classic and nuovo cucina. It has an unmatched wine selection that The Wine Spectator recently honored with its "Best of Award of Excellence." In the decade since its inception, Diamond's has been pleasing patrons and restaurant reviewers with its beguiling antipasti, creative pastas and splendid main dishes. From 1984 to 1993, its food and service were rated "excellent" by The Times of Trenton, and it was considered "one of the best restaurants in Trenton" in The New York Times, New Jersey section.

GARLIC BREAD FORMAGGIO

INGREDIENTS

- 2 garlic cloves, minced
- 4 tablespoons extra virgin olive oil
- 1 loaf French bread
- 2 tablespoons butter
- 1 ounce bleu cheese, crumbled (about 3 tablespoons)
- 1 ounce Swiss cheese, finely grated (about 3 tablespoons)
- 1 ounce mozzarella cheese, coarsely grated (about 3 tablespoons)
- 1 ounce parmigiana cheese, finely grated (about 5 tablespoons)
- 1/2 cup heavy cream
- 1/2 teaspoon dijon mustard

PREPARATION

Combine the garlic and the olive oil. Cut bread in 1/2 lengthwise and brush the cut sides of each 1/2 with olive oil mixture.

Melt butter in heavy saucepan over low heat. Add all the cheeses and cook mixture, stirring, until they are melted. Whisk in the cream, heated, and the mustard. Simmer the mixture, whisking for 5 minutes, or until it is creamy.

Toast bread under a broiler until it is golden brown and crispy. Cut into 2" wide strips and coat it evenly with cheese sauce. Serve immediately.

CHEF'S SUGGESTED MENU

Garlic Bread Formaggio

Soft Shell Crabs Francaise
(fresh soft shell crabs, dipped in egg batter and sautéed in butter with a hint of lemon)

Orecchiette
Tossed with Escarole and Black Olives
with Anchovies Sautéed in Extra Virgin Olive Oil,
with Garlic and Crushed Red Pepper

Filet Mignon Truffelini
(medallions of filet mignon sautéed in olive oil with garlic and fresh, sliced mushrooms; finished with shaved black truffles; served with broccoli rabe, porcini mushrooms and beer batter Vidalia onion rings)

Tiramisu

The Dining Room at The Hilton

AMERICAN / CONTEMPORARY

Dinner Tuesday – Saturday
Sunday Brunch in The Terrace

Live Jazz in The Retreat
Friday Evening
Live Band & Dancing in
The Retreat Saturday Evening

Elegant Corporate Meeting
& Party Facilities

Private Room in the Dining Room

Wine Maker & Tasting Dinners

Accepts Diners Club and Other
Major Credit Cards

41 JFK Parkway
Short Hills, NJ
201.379.0100

The strikingly handsome flagship restaurant of The Hilton at Short Hills, aptly named The Dining Room, is the setting for a world class dining experience that is rated "Excellent" by *The New York Times*, and honored with four stars by *The Star Ledger*. ❧ The culinary cornerstone of this luxurious restaurant is the artistic, imaginative cuisine of Anthony Demes, formerly of Maxime's in Manhattan. ❧ His sophisticated new American and neoclassical dishes are masterfully matched by a multiplicity of splendid wines, and proficiently served by a friendly staff conversant with the elegant cookery. ❧ Such dining experiences, enhanced by sophisticated harp music, create enduring memories. ❧ Little wonder The Hilton at Short Hills is the only "Five Diamond Hotel" in the New York metro area, and that its Dining Room is assessed "Best Restaurant in Northern New Jersey" by *New Jersey Monthly*.

Chilled Tiger Prawns

WITH FAVA BEAN SALAD,
SPICY CITRUS VINAIGRETTE

Ingredients

For Tiger Prawns:
6 cups court bouillon

8 Tiger Prawns (large shrimp, less than 10 per pound may be substituted)

For spicy citrus vinaigrette:
1/4 cup orange concentrate (1/2 cup fresh orange juice boiled until reduced by half)

1/4 cup lime juice

1/4 cup raspberry vinegar

2 teaspoons spicy sesame oil

1/2 cup vegetable oil

For the fava bean salad:
1 1/2 cups fava beans, blanched, shelled

1/2 cup tomato concasse (about 4 plum tomatoes, peeled, seeded and diced)

2 teaspoons red onions, diced (about 1/4 red onion)

Salt and pepper to taste

Preparation

Make the shrimp: Bring the court bouillon to a boil over medium heat. Poach the shrimp until they turn pink and are just cooked (about 2 to 3 minutes). Remove shells and veins and reserve in a bowl, covered with plastic wrap, in a refrigerator.

Make the vinaigrette: Place the orange concentrate, lime juice and raspberry vinegar in an earthenware pot. Bring to a boil over medium heat and simmer for 2 minutes. Place in a blender and blend. Add the sesame and vegetable oil slowly while the blender is running until fully incorporated.

Make the fava bean salad: Combine the fava beans with the tomato concasse and red onions in a bowl. Add the vinaigrette, plus salt and pepper to taste, and allow to marinate for 1 hour. Drain and reserve excess vinaigrette.

Assemble: Press the fava bean salad in round mold, invert in the center of a plate and unmold. Place chilled Tiger Prawns on top of the salad and drizzle with reserved vinaigrette. Garnish plate with greens and serve. Serves 2.

Chef's Suggested Menu

Warm Belon Oysters and Razor Clams
with Black Walnut-Chive Oil

Seared Scallops and Periwinkles
with Baby Fennel
and Porcini Butter Sauce

Chilled Tiger Prawns
with Fava Bean Salad
and Spicy Citrus Vinaigrette

Maine Lobster with
Creamy Rosemary Polenta,
Fried Celery and
Vidalia Onion Vinaigrette

Chilled Fruit Broth
with Sweet Seaweed and
Key Lime Sorbet

We Welcome

THE EBBITT ROOM

AMERICAN/CONTEMPORARY

Dinner Every Day
Saturday & Sunday Brunch

Valet Parking Weekend & in Season

Piano Music Weekends & in Season

Elegant Party & Wedding Facilities
Corporate Conference Facilities

24 Individually Decorated
Guest Rooms

Continental Breakfast for
Overnight Guests

Accepts Diners Club and Other
Major Credit Cards

VIRGINIA HOTEL
25 JACKSON STREET
CAPE MAY, NJ
609.884.5700

SELECTED WINNER OF *NEW JERSEY MONTHLY'S* 1993 READERS' CHOICE AWARD AS "BEST OF THE BEST" AND "BEST HOTEL RESTAURANT," THE CAPTIVATING EBBITT ROOM AT THE VIRGINIA HOTEL PROVIDES HOUSE GUESTS AND VISITORS WITH A FINE DINING EXPERIENCE IN VICTORIAN CAPE MAY, NEW JERSEY. A DISTINCTIVE PLACE FOR A WEEKEND GETAWAY OR CORPORATE FUNCTION, THE VIRGINIA HOTEL, CIRCA 1879, WAS RECENTLY RETURNED TO ITS ORIGINAL GRANDEUR AND UPDATED WITH MODERN AMENITIES, TO BECOME A DELIGHTFUL 24-ROOM, LUXURY INN AND GOURMET RESTAURANT. THE EBBITT ROOM'S PROVOCATIVE CUISINE IS AN ENLIGHTENED BLEND OF CONTEMPORARY AMERICAN FARE COMBINED WITH FRENCH, ITALIAN AND ORIENTAL ACCENTS. DELICACIES, SUCH AS ASIAN NOODLE SALAD WITH HONEY, SOY AND RASPBERRY VINAIGRETTE AND SMOKED CHICKEN, ARE SKILLFULLY SERVED AND ACCOMPANIED BY A DIVERSE SELECTION OF MODERATELY PRICED WINES.

Rainbow Trout in a Hazelnut Crust

Ingredients

- 4-6 ounces hazelnuts (1 1/3 cups in shell)
- 10 ounces trout fillet (2 sides of a trout)
- 2 tablespoons vegetable oil
- 2 ounces fresh spinach, cleaned and squeezed dry in paper towel (2 cups packed)
- Oil for deep frying (2 cups)

Roast Garlic:
- Mirepoix made of 1/3 cup each minced shallot, celery, carrot
- 2 tablespoons unsalted butter
- 1 sprig fresh thyme
- 1 bay leaf
- 6 crushed peppercorns
- 2 1/2 tablespoons tomato paste
- 2/3 cup burgundy wine
- 3 cups prepared demi-glace
- 1 whole bulb garlic, cloves separated
- 4 tablespoons cold unsalted butter cut into small pieces
- Salt and pepper

Preparation

Toast hazelnuts for 15 minutes at 350° F. Cool, peel and chop in food processor until as fine as flour. Dredge the trout in hazelnut flour and sauté in vegetable oil over medium-high heat, turning, until golden brown on both sides (about 3 1/2 minutes). Deep fry spinach at 350° F until crisp (only 10 to 15 seconds to keep green). Place trout in the center of a large plate encircled by the spinach. Drizzle 3 ounces of roast garlic sauce around the trout and serve immediately.

Roast Garlic: (Enough sauce for four trout.) Cook mirepoix in butter combined with thyme, bay leaf and peppercorns in a heavy bottom sauce pan over low heat until vegetables are very soft (15 minutes). Add the tomato paste and wine and bring to a boil. Cook until the sauce is reduced to 1/2 cup (about 5 minutes). Add demi-glace and cook, continually skimming the surface until the sauce is thick enough to coat the back of a spoon (about 30 minutes) Strain the sauce. Roast the garlic cloves in a preheated oven at 300° F until they are soft. Peel the garlic and pureé into the strained sauce. Reduce the heat to moderately low and whisk in the butter, one piece at a time, lifting the skillet from the heat occasionally to cool the mixture. Add each new piece of butter before the previous one has melted completely. The sauce should not get hot enough to liquify. It should be thin enough to coat the back of a spoon. Add salt and pepper to taste. Serves 4.

Chef's Suggested Menu

Smoked Salmon & Potato Napoleon, Lemon Cream, Chive Oil

Rainbow Trout in Hazelnut Crust, Lobster-Chive Sauce; Quick Fried Spinach

Roast Chicken Breast Stuffed with Spinach, Mushrooms and Pecorino

Roast Rack of Lamb with White Bean Cassoulet and Honey-Thyme Jus

Seasonal Greens with Stilton Cheese, Granny Smith Apples, Toasted Walnuts, Port Wine Vinaigrette

THE EBBITT ROOM

We Welcome

ECCOLA ITALIAN BISTRO

ITALIAN

Lunch Monday – Saturday
Dinner Every Day

Proper Casual Attire

Valet Parking

Distinctive Complete Take-Out Lunch or Dinner in Microwave Dishes (with Eating Utensils) for Office or Home

Accepts Diners Club and Other Major Credit Cards

1082 ROUTE 46 WEST
PARSIPPANY, NJ
201.334.8211

NENAD AND JANET TAMBURIN'S ECCOLA ITALIAN BISTRO IS A STRIKINGLY HANDSOME COSMOPOLITAN RESTAURANT WITH AN AWARD-WINNING INTERIOR DESIGN THAT'S COUPLED WITH FOOD AND SERVICE EVERY BIT AS ENTICING AS THE DECOR. "DESIGNER" PIZZA FROM A WOOD-BURNING ITALIAN OVEN, DAZZLING ANTIPASTI, GLORIOUS PASTAS MADE ON THE PREMISES AND REGIONAL DISHES EMANATING FROM ECCOLA'S STYLISH OPEN KITCHEN ARE TOP-DRAWER VERSIONS OF GENUINE ITALIAN TRATTORIA-STYLE CUISINE. ECCOLA'S CHEF-OWNER NENAD TAMBURIN IS A CHARMER, GREETING GUESTS FROM THE FRONT OF THE OPEN KITCHEN WHERE HE SUPERVISES ALL THE COOKERY. HIS WIFE, JANET, A FRENCH-TRAINED PATISSIERE-EXTRAORDINAIRE AND HOSTESS, PREPARES ECCOLA'S VOLUPTUOUS DESSERTS THAT MAKE DIETERS LOSE ALL RESOLVE. A MEAL AT ECCOLA IS LIKE DINING IN ITALY.

Pappardelle Taormina

Ingredients

- 2 pounds pappardelle
- 2 teaspoons vegetable oil
- 2 cloves garlic, sliced thin
- 4 fresh sage leaves
- 3 ounces olive oil
- 1 pound fresh white button mushrooms, quartered
- 12 ounces prosciutto, sliced thin, cut in julienne strips
- 1 pound of shrimp, peeled and deveined
- 1/2 cup dry white wine
- 2 cups marinara style tomato sauce
- 2 cups heavy cream
- 1 cup fresh peas
- 1 pinch salt
- 1 pinch fresh milled pepper
- 1 pinch garlic powder

Preparation

Cook pappardelle in 8 quarts of boiling salted water until al dente (about 7 minutes for dry, 3 minutes for fresh). Drain, toss with vegetable oil to prevent sticking, and reserve.

In a large skillet, sauté the garlic and sage in the olive oil over medium heat. When the garlic is lightly browned, add the mushrooms and cook, stirring 2 to 3 minutes. Add the prosciutto and sauté 1 minute, stirring. Increase the heat to high, add the shrimp and sauté 1 minute, stirring. Add the white wine and when it begins to boil, add the marinara sauce and heavy cream. Mix well to incorporate. Add the peas and simmer for about 3 minutes or until sauce thickens. Add salt, pepper and garlic powder to taste. Keep the sauce warm over very low heat.

Add 1/3 of the sauce to another clean skillet. Heat over medium heat and add all the pasta to the sauce. Toss the pasta until it is evenly coated. Place 1/4 of the pasta in each of 4 plates. Distribute the rest of the sauce evenly over the pasta on each plate. Serve immediately. Serves 4.

Chef's Suggested Menu

Grilled Calamari
(char-grilled marinated calamari au jus)

Pappardelle Taormina

Penne alla Russa
(diagonal-cut macaroni flavored with garlic, vodka, tomato and cream)

Petto di Pollo,
Saltato Con Funghi Selvatici
(breast of chicken, sautéed with wild mushrooms)

Osso Buco Con Salsa di Verduna
(braised veal shanks with light brown vegetable sauce)

Raspberry Rhapsody

We Welcome

The Farmingdale House

ITALIAN

Dinner only Tuesday – Sunday
Jackets Required
Valet Parking on Weekends
Accepts Diners Club and Other Major Credit Cards

105 Academy Street
Farmingdale, NJ
908.938.7951

Toni Froio, proprietor-chef of the highly acclaimed Farmingdale House, is one of the few great Italian woman chefs tantalizing American taste buds with genuine readings of the provocative fare of her homeland. Her masterful creations, like her signature dish of grilled jumbo shrimp wrapped in fresh mozzarella and pancetta (Gamberi Luciana) and filetto di vitello vecchia Modena (tenderloin of snowy veal coupled with raisins, cheese and porcini mushrooms in puff pastry) are a small sampling of the distinguished dishes that win raves at this cozy dining spot. The *Zagat Tri-State Restaurant Survey* rated the Farmingdale House the "Top Northern Italian" and it merited "Four Stars" in the *Asbury Park Press*. "Excellent" was the overall appraisal of *New Jersey Monthly* restaurant critics and they labeled it "a treasure"– while a poll of its readers chose it "Best of the Best".

Gamberi Luciana

Ingredients

- 6 slices mozzarella cheese, 1" by 3"
- 6 jumbo shrimp, peeled, deveined and butterflied
- 6 slices pancetta, sliced very thin
- 1 tablespoon plus 1 teaspoon butter
- 1/2 teaspoon shallots, finely chopped
- 1/2 teaspoon capers, finely chopped
- 1/4 cup dry white wine
- A splash of Pernod (about 1/4 teaspoon)
- Fresh parsley, chopped (about 2 tablespoons)

Preparation

Place a slice of cheese on the butterflied side of each shrimp and wrap each one with 1 slice of pancetta. Cover the tail of the shrimp to prevent burning. Place on a baking sheet and bake in a preheated oven at 400° F for 8 minutes. In a saucepan heat 1 tablespoon of the butter over moderate heat until melted. Add the shallots and capers and sauté until shallots are translucent. Add the dry white wine and bring to a boil. Bring all to boil until volume is reduced by half. Add the Pernod and remove from the heat. Whisk into the sauce 1 teaspoon of the butter and sprinkle it with the parsley. Pour the sauce in the center of a large warm plate. Arrange the cooked shrimp over the sauce. Garnish the plate with a few leaves of frisee.

Chef's Suggested Menu

Gamberi Luciana

Cappellacci Ripieni di Zucca con Salsiccia e Funghi Porcini
(cappellacci pasta filled with squash, sausage and porcini mushrooms)

Ruchetta e Pomodoro con Olio d'Oliva e Aceto Balsamico
(wild ruchetta and tomatoes with olive oil and balsamic vinegar)

Vitello Mignon alla Vecchia Modena
(medallions of tenderloin of veal with cream cheese, prosciutto and scallions in a wine and black mushroom sauce)

Torta al Cioccolato e Mandorie
(chocolate and almond gateau)

The Farmingdale House

We Welcome
Diners Club International

40 Main Street

AMERICAN/CONTEMPORARY

Lunch Tuesday – Friday
Dinner Tuesday – Saturday

Proper Attire

Music Tuesday Nights

Private Parties & Catering

Next Door Cafe Main:
Open 7 Days Lunch & Dinner
Casual Dining & Bar
No Reservations – Casual Attire
Music Thursday – Saturday

Accepts Diners Club and Other
Major Credit Cards

40 Main Street
Millburn, NJ
201.376.4444

Located in the center of Millburn Township, only a five-minute walk from the historic Paper Mill Playhouse, 40 Main Street opened in 1984. Shortly thereafter, its gourmet contemporary American cuisine was acclaimed by leading restaurant reviewers, including *The New York Times*, *Mobil Travel Guide* (three stars), *New Jersey Monthly*, *The Star-Ledger*, *Daily Record* and *New Jersey Goodlife*. The 1993 *Zagat Tri-State Restaurant Survey* listed 40 Main Street among "Northern New Jersey's Most Popular Restaurants." The rave reviews reflect its skillfully executed, inventive cuisine based on respectfully cooked, prime fresh ingredients and sauces with natural flavors. The sophisticated food is complemented by a distinguished service staff and a substantial selection of splendid wines which are offered by the glass, half-bottle and bottle.

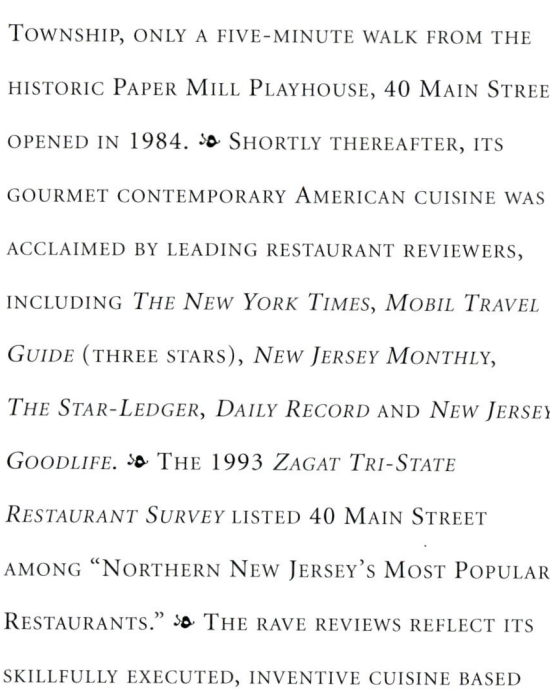

GRILLED SHRIMP WITH SALSA AND SWEET POTATO CHIPS

INGREDIENTS

For the salsa:
2 red peppers, roasted

2 green peppers, roasted

2 yellow peppers, roasted

1 red onion

4 beef steak tomatoes, peeled

1/2 cup champagne vinegar

1 cup olive oil

1 dash Worcestershire sauce

5 dashes Tabasco sauce

Salt and pepper

3 tablespoons chopped cilantro

For the sweet potato chips:
3 sweet potatoes, sliced thinly

Vegetable (or soybean) oil for deep frying

For the shrimp:
3 pounds shrimp (16 - 20 per pound), peeled and deveined

1/2 cup olive oil

Salt and pepper

PREPARATION

Make the salsa: Dice roasted and peeled peppers, onion and tomatoes and place them in a large non-reactive (glass or stainless steel) bowl. Add all the liquid ingredients and mix well to combine. Season the blend with salt and pepper to taste. Add cilantro and mix well. Let the mixture sit in a refrigerator, covered for 24 hours. Recipe makes 5 cups. Any excess may be used as a dip with chips.

Make the sweet potato chips: Deep fry potatoes at 275° F until crisp. Remove and drain them. Blot them dry of oil on paper towels. (Note, the lower frying temperature produces a wonderful orange color chip.)

Make the grilled shrimp: Coat shrimp with olive oil and lightly sprinkle with salt and pepper. Grill shrimp over high heat until lightly brown on both sides (about 3 minutes).

Assemble: Place the shrimp on a platter surrounded by sweet potato chips and bowl of salsa for dipping. Serves 12.

CHEF'S SUGGESTED MENU

∽

Marinated Grilled Shrimp with Homemade Sweet Potato Chips

Seared Australian Lamb Loin with Morels, Herb Polenta and Natural Reduction

Fresh Tagliatelli with Rock Shrimp; Sun-dried Tomatoes in a Lemon, Garlic and Chive Sauce

Grilled Tenderloin of Beef with Grilled Vidalia Onions and Reggiano Potatoes

White Chocolate Mousse with Fresh Raspberries

∽

FOUR SEAS, CUISINES OF CHINA

CHINESE

Dinner Tuesday – Sunday
Dim Sum Brunch
Saturday & Sunday Noon – 3 PM
Lunch Tuesday – Friday

Jackets Required in Special Section,
Proper Dress in Other Rooms

Self-Parking

Party Facilities
Special Movie/Dinner Package

Take-Out Service and
Off Premise Catering

Accepts Diners Club and Other
Major Credit Cards

24 MAIN STREET
MADISON, NJ
201.822.2899

In 1988 the Four Seas, Cuisines of China was the pacesetter that introduced cosmopolitan Chinese dining to New Jersey. Its Westernized quarters, which feature decorative touches like a fireplace, skylights and a profusion of greenery, are a far cry from the usual New Jersey Chinese restaurant. However, it's the provocative cuisine – a true taste of China's four tantalizing culinary regions – coupled with an intelligent wine selection that makes dining at the Four Seas an uncommon adventure. Celebrated fare like Peking duck and crispy sea bass are impressive. Imaginative options like firecracker beef, duck sautéed with preserved ginger and salmon sautéed in an elegant white sauce are splendid introductions to the talents and diversity of the exceptional chefs of the Four Seas.

Jade Chicken

Ingredients

1 1/2 fresh boneless, skinless chicken breasts, sliced into 2" by 1/4" julienne strips (about 1 pound)

Marinade for Chicken:
1/2 teaspoon light soy sauce

1 large egg white

1 teaspoon cornstarch

Oil for deep frying

1/2 cup carrots, peeled and shredded into julienne strips

1 cup fresh snow peas (each pea cut into 3 pieces length wise)

1 teaspoon fresh grated ginger root

Seasoning Sauce:
Mix following ingredients well and reserve:

1 teaspoon light soy sauce

1 teaspoon sesame oil

1 teaspoon Chinese rice wine (dry sherry optional)

1 teaspoon sugar

1 teaspoon cornstarch

1/2 teaspoon salt

Steamed long grain rice as an accompaniment

Preparation

Coat the chicken with marinade in covered bowl. Marinate for 30 minutes to an hour.

In a wok or large skillet, heat 1" of the oil to 375° F. Add the chicken and fry, stirring 1 to 2 minutes until chicken is white and opaque. Transfer the chicken with a slotted spoon to a plate and pour off all but 2 tablespoons of the oil from the wok. Add the carrots, snow peas and ginger root and stir fry over high heat for 1 minute. Add the seasoning sauce and bring mixture to a boil, stirring. Return the chicken to the wok and cook mixture until it is heated through.

Serve Jade Chicken with steamed rice. Serves 3 as main course or 4 to 6 as part of multi-course Chinese meal.

Chef's Suggested Menu

Cold Spinach Noodles
(tossed in a sesame oil vinaigrette with sliced sea scallops, baby shrimp, slivered bamboo shoots and scallions)

Jade Chicken

Soft Shell Crabs in Ginger Sauce
(crisply fried soft shell crabs bathed with a gingery, moderately-spicy sauce accented with scallion shreds)

Cantonese Roast Duck
(slices of savory roast duck awash in a hauntingly fragrant brown sauce and garnished with preserved ginger)

Firecracker Beef
(julienne shreds of beef glazed with a sweet-and-spicy garlic sauce accented by slivers of carrots and snow peas)

Chinese Multi-Treasure Rice Pudding
(warm glutinous rice pudding studded with candied fruits, raisins and sweet red bean paste)

Four Seas

The Frog and The Peach

AMERICAN

Lunch Monday – Friday
Dinner Every Day
Free Parking
Outdoor Dining Facilities
Corporate House Accounts
Custom Party Planning
Regular Lunch & Dinner Menu
at the Bar
Beer & Wine Tasting at the Bar
Accepts Diners Club and Other
Major Credit Cards

Corner of Hiram and
Dennis Streets
New Brunswick, NJ
908.846.3216

The Frog and The Peach – established by restaurateur Jim Black and Chef Elizabeth Alger in 1983 – rapidly gained notoriety as an innovative American culinary treasure. ✒ The *Zagat Tri-State Restaurant Survey* rated The Frog and The Peach "Top American (Contemporary)" and ranked it among the top ten in its list of "Northern New Jersey's Most Popular Restaurants". ✒ It was voted "Best of the Best" for six consecutive years in *New Jersey Monthly's* Readers' Choice Awards and it was rated "excellent" in the New Jersey section of *The New York Times*. ✒ Situated one block south of the Hyatt, a short walk from Johnson & Johnson Corporate Headquarters and two blocks from the State Cultural Center, The Frog and the Peach is an ideal spot for business lunch, dinner or a special night out.

Sautéed Quail Breast and Leg Dumplings
with Rhubarb Black Currant Compoté

Ingredients

6 whole quail

Salt and freshly milled white pepper to taste

1 egg yolk mixed with water to make egg wash

12 3" squares of fresh pasta (wonton skins optional)

Duck fat for sautéing (or olive oil)

For the sauce:

3 cups port wine

1 cup sugar

1 cup rice wine vinegar

6 stalks fresh rhubarb, cut into 3" x 1/4" strips

1/2 cup sun-dried black currants

3 tablespoons cold, unsalted butter, cut into 6 pieces

6 sprigs of chervil

Preparation

Break down quail legs. Remove thigh bone making a long incision lengthwise and keeping meat intact. Bone breast, leaving wing attached. Season leg meat with fresh milled white pepper, place in center of an egg washed square of pasta (original joint down, leg facing vertically up) and wrap (like beggar's purse) around leg leaving some leg meat exposed at top.

Deep fry leg dumplings at 350° F until golden brown (about 5 minutes). Season breasts with salt and fresh milled white pepper and sauté in duck fat (olive oil optional) over high heat until rare to medium rare.

In a saucepan, simmer the port wine until it is reduced to 1 cup. Add the sugar and vinegar until reduced by half. Add rhubarb and currants with liquid and simmer over high heat for 2 minutes. Reduce the heat to moderately low and whisk in the butter, one piece at a time, lifting the skillet from the heat occasionally to cool the mixture. Add each new piece of butter before the previous one has melted completely. The sauce should not get hot enough to liquify. It should be thin enough to coat the back of a spoon.

Spoon sauce onto warm plates dividing equally and arrange breasts and leg dumplings on sauce. Garnish with chervil sprigs. Serves 6.

Chef's Suggested Menu

Pastrami-Cured Salmon
with Caraway Rye Crackers
in Caper Watercress Dressing

Spinach Salad
with Sliced Aged Goat Cheese,
Herb-Cured Black Olives,
Roasted Peppers
and Crisp Onion Rings

Sautéed Breast of Quail
and Fried Quail Leg Dumplings in
a Compoté of Port Wine,
Poached Rhubarb and Sun-Dried
Black Currants in Natural Juices

Grilled Tenderloin of Beef
with Fried Onion Rings,
Grilled Portobello Mushrooms,
Roast Shallot Ravioli and Salsify in a
Roast Shallot Demi-Glace

Warm Fruit Tart
in an Almond Filo Pastry with
Star Anise Ice Cream
and an Orange Muscat Caramel Sauce

Fromagerie

FRENCH

Lunch Monday – Friday
Dinner Every Day

Jackets Required

Valet Parking

Elegant Party Facilities

Private Function Rooms Available

Accepts Diners Club and Other
Major Credit Cards

26 Ridge Road
Rumson, NJ
908.842.8088

Established by brothers Hubert and Markus Peter in 1972 in a spacious private home, the Fromagerie is noted for its classic French cuisine with a contemporary panache. Dishes are skillfully served in a warm, romantic setting and paired with an award-winning selection of wines. Since 1986, the Fromagerie has been selected for the highest award *New Jersey Monthly* readers bestow on restaurants, the "Best of the Best". It has also been rated as one of the most popular restaurant in Northern New Jersey, one of the top three for French Classic Cuisine, and accorded premiere ratings for decor and service by the *Zagat Tri-State Restaurant Survey*. However, that isn't surprising to the Peters, for their restaurant has consistently been recognized by gastronomes and the restaurant press corps as one of the finest French restaurants in New Jersey since they opened the doors more than 20 years ago.

Red Snapper and Shellfish Matelote

Ingredients

3 tablespoons olive oil

1 onion, diced (3/4 cups)

1/2 carrot, diced (1/4 cup)

1/2 fennel bulb, diced (1/2 cup)

1/2 parsnip, peeled and diced (1/3 cup)

1/2 potato, diced (2/3 cup)

1 cup dry white wine

4 cups fish stock

1 sprig tarragon

1 sprig thyme

1 teaspoon fine herbs

8 clams in shell

1 pound lobster (cut lengthwise)

7 ounce fillet red snapper

8 mussels in shell

4 shrimp, peeled and deveined

1 tomato concasse (peeled, seeded, chopped and sautéed in 1 tablespoon of butter with 2 tablespoons of chopped onions)

1 sprig parsley, chopped

Salt and pepper to taste

Garlic

Saffron rouille

Preparation

Add olive oil to a preheated heavy soup pot over low heat. Add onion, carrot, fennel, parsnip and potato and cook over low heat with occasional mixing for about 20 minutes (sweat vegetables).

Add white wine and allow to boil until almost dry (5 to 7 minutes). Add fish stock with tarragon, thyme and fine herbs and simmer over low heat for 20 minutes. Increase heat to medium, add clams and lobster and cook for 2 minutes. Then add red snapper and mussels and cook for 1 minute. Then add shrimp and cook for 2 minutes longer. Transfer to a heated large soup tureen, add tomato concasse and parsley. Add salt and pepper to taste and serve with garlic, put saffron rouille on the side. Makes 2 large portions.

Chef's Suggested Menu

House Smoked Salmon
on Potato Pancake
with Dill-Accented Cream Sauce
and Salmon Caviar

Marinated Portobello Mushrooms
with Roasted Peppers,
Mozzarella Au Gratin and
Balsamic Vinaigrette

Red Snapper and Shellfish Matelote
with Shrimp, Mussels
and Lobster in a White Wine Broth

Assorted Baby Greens
with Toasted Pine Nuts, Roquefort
Cheese and Sliced Pears,
Tossed with a Champagne Vinaigrette

Multi-layered Espresso Mousse Cake
with Sauce Anglaise
and Chocolate Triangles

Fromagerie

GIRAFE

AMERICAN

Dinner Monday – Saturday
Lunch Monday – Friday

Jackets Required
for Gentlemen in Evenings

On-Site Parking

Private Party Facilities for
Weddings, Rehearsal Dinners,
Social Parties and Corporate Events

Accepts Diners Club and Other
Major Credit Cards

95 Morristown Road
Basking Ridge, NJ
908.221.0017

The Girafe restaurant, located in Basking Ridge, proudly celebrates its 12th anniversary. This elegant, romantic and sophisticated restaurant offers creative American cuisine in a comfortably formal and artistic setting. Rated "excellent" by *The New York Times* and recipient of *The Wine Spectator's* Award of Excellence, it's no surprise that the Girafe is considered one of the premier restaurants in the state. Proprietors John Rader, Chef Barry Squier and maitre d' Kenneth Woodin, strive to offer captivating cuisine graciously served in their elegant main dining room, wood-paneled private board room and spacious banquet facilities. This dedication to quality and value makes the Girafe the perfect solution for social and corporate entertaining.

Black Bean Soup with Andouille Sausage

Ingredients

For the soup:
- 2 onions, diced (about 2 cups)
- 3 large cloves of garlic, sliced
- 1 green pepper, diced (about 3/4 cup)
- 1 jalapeno pepper with seeds, chopped
- 1/4 cup extra virgin olive oil
- 2 pounds black beans soaked in water to cover overnight
- Homemade or low sodium canned chicken stock to cover (about 7 to 9 cups)
- 1 carrot, diced
- 1 stalk celery, diced (about 1/3 cup)
- 1 teaspoon dried oregano
- 1/2 teaspoon thyme
- 1/2 teaspoon basil
- 1 teaspoon ground cumin
- 2 bay leaves
- 1 16 ounce can chopped tomatoes
- 1 teaspoon pink peppercorns

For the seasoning:
- 8 ounces andouille sausage, ground
- Juice of 2 oranges
- 2 tablespoons cilantro
- 1 ounce balsamic vinegar
- Tabasco sauce to taste
- Salt to taste

Preparation

Sweat (cook over low heat) onions, garlic and peppers in virgin olive oil. Add the black beans, drained, seven cups of the chicken stock and the remaining ingredients. Simmer over low heat until beans are very soft (about 1 to 2 hours). Add additional chicken stock as needed. Pureé the soup in batches in a blender or food processor and place in a soup pot.

Add seasonings and reheat over medium low heat and simmer for 3 minutes. Garnish with finely chopped onions, fresh cilantro and hard cooked eggs before serving.

Chef's Suggested Menu

~

Black Bean Soup with Andouille Sausage

Chilled Angel Hair Pasta with Radicchio, Arugula, Tomato, Herb-Infused Olive Oil and Rive Vinegar

Pan Roasted Skate with Young Lettuce and an Orange-Cumin Vinaigrette, Mango Compote and Crispy Lace Potatoes

Medallions of South Texas Antelope with a Potato-Leek Wedge, Calypso Beans, Caramelized Pearl Onions and a Raspberry Cabernet Sauce

Blackberry Silk Tartlet, Creme Fraiche Lattice

~

The Grand Cafe

FRENCH / CONTEMPORARY

Lunch Monday – Friday
Dinner Monday – Saturday
Closed Sundays

Proper Attire Please

Self-Parking

Piano Music Weekends

Elegant Corporate Meeting
& Party Facilities

Off Premise Catering

Accepts Diners Club and Other
Major Credit Cards

---

42 Washington Street
Morristown, NJ
201.540.9444

The Grand Cafe, created by Desmond Lloyd and Jack Baker almost a decade ago, has developed into one of the finest deluxe restaurants in New Jersey. That appraisal is shared in the *Zagat Tri-State Restaurant Survey* by listing the Grand Cafe as one of the most popular restaurants, plus top listings for food, overall decor and service. The Grand Cafe was also rated "excellent" and was awarded three stars in "New Jersey's Best Dining" by the restaurant reviewers of *The New York Times*, New Jersey Section. The chic restaurant, which attracts a highly charged, cosmopolitan, corporate and private clientele, features brilliant cookery by Michael Guessefeld, exemplary service and top-value wines from the Cafe's extensive, discriminating selection of French and California bottles.

CRISPY GOAT CHEESE DUMPLINGS
WITH MEDITERRANEAN STYLE VINAIGRETTE

INGREDIENTS

For the vinaigrette:
1 cup extra virgin olive oil
1/3 cup balsamic vinegar
3 tablespoons red pepper
3 tablespoons black olives
3 tablespoons red onions
3 tablespoons sun-dried tomatoes (oil packed)
2 tablespoons fresh cilantro
2 tablespoons fresh parsley
2 tablespoons fresh basil
1 teaspoon garlic, chopped

For the carrot garnish:
1 large carrot, julienne strips
2 teaspoons fresh tarragon, chopped
1 tablespoon extra virgin olive oil
1 teaspoon balsamic vinegar

For the dumplings:
14 ounces goat cheese
1 bunch of chives, diced (about 4 tablespoons)
Salt and pepper
24 3" square sheets fresh pasta (spring roll or wonton wrappers optional)
2 whole beaten eggs for wash
Vegetable oil for deep frying

PREPARATION

Make the vinaigrette: Finely chop, then whisk the ingredients; reserve. Whisk again just before using.

Make the carrot garnish: Blanch carrot in boiling water quickly, keeping it crunchy (about 15 seconds). Remove and refresh in an ice water bath. Dry well over paper towels. Sprinkle carrots with tarragon, oil and vinegar and reserve.

Make the dumplings: Place goat cheese and chives in a food processor and pureé until smooth. Add salt and pepper to taste. Spoon a teaspoon of goat cheese filling in center of pasta and lightly brush edges with egg wash. Bring the corners together to form pockets, pressing the pasta so it seals very well. Deep fry in 3" of 360° F vegetable oil for about 3 minutes until golden brown. Remove gently, drain and dry over paper towels.

Assemble: Place 4 dumplings around the outside of each of 6 plates. Place bunches of the carrot garnish between the dumplings and a small pond of vinaigrette in the center of the plate. Serve immediately. Serves 6.

CHEF'S SUGGESTED MENU

Crispy Goat Cheese Dumplings with a Mediterranean Style Vinaigrette

Warm Lobster Salad with Shiitake Mushrooms and Sherry Vinaigrette on a Bed of Angel Hair Pasta

Escalopes of Atlantic Salmon with Pesto Sauce, Salsa, Creamy Mashed Potatoes and Parmesan Chips

Roasted Chicken with Country Style Cabbage and Glazed Baby Onions Dotted with Demi-Glace and Carrot-Fennel Seed Essence

Fresh Seasonal Fruit Tart

HARLEQUIN CAFE

ITALIAN

Lunch Monday – Friday
Dinner Monday – Saturday
Closed Sundays but Available
for Elegant Private Parties

Proper Attire Please

Self-Parking

Piano Music Tuesday – Saturday

Off Premise Catering

Accepts Diners Club and Other
Major Credit Cards

322 SOUTH MAIN STREET
WHARTON, NJ
201.366.8154

Antonio and Marco de Filippis transformed a mundane Wharton saloon into an upscale, urbane Italian bistro in 1988 and named it Harlequin Cafe. It opened to rave reviews because of Marco's skillfully crafted, creative dishes, Antonio's charming personality and the competence of his proficient, unpretentious servers. The de Filippis, who didn't sit on their instant success, haven't stopped upgrading the appearance of the dining room and fine tuning all phases of their operation. The ambiance of the cafe mirrors a quaint Soho bistro. The walls are hung with attractive Harlequin-theme oil paintings, and classic and jazz piano music provides an unobtrusive backdrop. The kitchen continually creates innovative dishes using the best ingredients and Franco-Italian techniques that spotlight their natural tastes.

Bistecca Nordestino

Ingredients

For the sauce:
1/4 cup extra virgin olive oil

2 cloves fresh garlic, sliced thin

1 red pepper, cut into julienne strips

1 green pepper, cut into julienne strips

4 sun-dried tomatoes (packed in oil) cut in julienne strips

1/4 cup balsamic vinegar

1/4 cup veal stock (chicken stock optional)

Sugar to taste (about 1 teaspoon)

For the steak:
2 boneless shell steaks, cut 1" thick

2 tablespoons extra virgin olive oil

A pinch of dried Italian hot pepper flakes to taste

Minced fresh parsley

Salt to taste

Preparation

Make the sauce: Heat 1/4 cup olive oil in large skillet over high heat. Add the garlic, peppers and sun-dried tomatoes and sauté, stirring constantly, for about 2 minutes. Add the vinegar and veal stock and boil the mixture until reduced by half. Keep warm.

Make the steaks: Brush steaks with oil, sprinkle with dried pepper flakes, parsley and salt to taste. Allow steaks to stand for about 15 minutes. Broil steaks on oiled grill until desired degree (about 2 to 3 minutes per side for medium rare).

Assemble: Pour sauce over the steaks and serve immediately. Serves 2.

Chef's Suggested Menu

Gamberoni alla Monaco
(jumbo shrimp wrapped with Parma prosciutto and basil leaf, dipped in a dijon mustard infused vinaigrette and grilled)

Rigatoni Harlequin
(short grooved noodle tubes stuffed with mushroom mousse and tossed with a veal demi-glace accented with mascarpone cheese)

Bistecca Nordestino
(grilled center-cut strip sirloin covered with a sautéed blend of sun-dried tomatoes with green and red peppers accented with balsamic vinegar and extra virgin olive oil)

Sorbetto di Frutti
(homemade fresh fruit sorbet with fresh seasonal berries)

Highlawn Pavilion

AMERICAN

Closed Christmas Eve
Gentlemen: Jackets Please
Valet & Self-Parking
Piano Music in The Oyster Bar
Elegant Party Facilities
Outdoor Dining Facilities
Express Lunch Menu
Accepts Diners Club and Other Major Credit Cards

Eagle Rock Reservation
West Orange, NJ
201.731.DINE

Built in 1909, the Florentine-style building in Eagle Rock Reservation was enjoyed by visitors for many years as a scenic outlook with a spectacular view of the New York skyline. With its French rotisserie, wood-burning Italian brick oven and open-kitchen concept, Highlawn Pavilion offers "American Fare with European Flair." The sparkling Manhattan skyline view is surpassed only by its four-star cuisine, which has been featured in leading lifestyle magazines. Popular with Paper Mill Playhouse stars, Highlawn Pavilion offers pre-theater dining beginning at 5:30 p.m. The beautiful Oyster Bar, which offers light fare and express luncheons, features a pianist/singer Wednesday through Sunday evenings. Cocktails and al fresco dining on the cliff-top patio are offered May through October.

STRIPED BASS WITH AN ARTICHOKE CRUST

INGREDIENTS

6 artichokes (2 cups cooked)
1/2 cup olive oil
1 tablespoon shallots, chopped
1 tablespoon garlic, chopped
Kosher salt
Fresh milled white pepper
2 egg yolks

2 cups dried white bread crumbs
2 tablespoons Italian parsley, chopped
6 8 ounce fillets of farm raised striped bass (sea bass optional) with pin bones removed

PREPARATION

Cook the artichokes in 6 quarts of boiling salted water for 20 to 30 minutes (when outer leaves pull free from the heart, the chokes are sufficiently cooked). Remove and place them in iced water. Remove and discard all the outer leaves. Spoon out the thistle chokes from the hearts. Dice or coarsely chop the chokes in a food processor.

In a preheated sauté pan, add 1/4 cup of the oil, the shallots and garlic. Cook until transparent and golden (1 minute). Add the diced choke hearts and sauté for 1 minute, drawing all the moisture, until lightly golden (4 minutes). Transfer to a mixing bowl and season with kosher salt and white pepper to taste. Fold in egg yolks, then bread crumbs and chopped parsley and reserve.

In a very hot preheated skillet, add remaining oil in a skillet and place bass fillets in the pan, skin side up. Sear bass fillets golden brown on one side (about 1 to 2 minutes), remove and allow to cool to room temperature. Spread the artichoke blend evenly over the seared side of the fillets. Place the fillets in a non-stick baking pan and brown under a broiler (high heat) until golden brown.

Serve over a roast red pepper fillet with a little wilted arugula or atop a bed of chopped fresh tomatoes with basil. Serves 6.

CHEF'S SUGGESTED MENU

Assorted Shellfish Tray Shrimp, Oysters, Clams and Lobster Claws

House Smoked Salmon with Potato and Artichoke Pancake

Mixed Baby Greens with Vinaigrette

Striped Bass with an Artichoke Crust

Grilled Double Lamb Chops with Tuscan Bean Cakes

Fresh Fruit Tart with Sesame Crust

HIGHLAWN PAVILION

Iberia Peninsula

SPANISH/PORTUGUESE

Lunch Monday – Friday
Dinner Daily

Casual, Proper Attire

Self-Parking in a Private Parking Lot

Private Party Facilities

Accepts Diners Club and Other Major Credit Cards

69 Ferry Street
Newark, NJ
201.344.5611

The Iberia Peninsula is a large handsome restaurant with provocative food that outclasses its Ironbound counterparts. Some of the gastronomic highlights featured at this remarkable restaurant include a "Rodizio" (a cornucopia of barbecued meats) complemented by a myriad of masterfully prepared dishes that authentically represent the cuisines of Portugal and eastern part of Spain. Iberia's distinctive fare is complemented by a cordial, adept service staff coupled with a superior selection of Portuguese and Spanish wines and spirits that provide lots of superior options for knowledgeable penny-wise patrons. Dishes not to be missed include Iberia Peninsula's succulent clams in a savory garlic sauce, marvelous braised baby pheasant and its famous Rodizio. This magnificent conglomeration of marinated meats, skewered and grilled over hot coals, provide a bewitching culinary journey to Portugal you won't soon forget.

Carne de Porco a Alentejana

Ingredients

1/2 cup dry white wine

4 teaspoons sweet paprika

1 bay leaf

2 1/2 teaspoons salt

1/4 teaspoons black pepper, freshly ground

4 garlic cloves, crushed

2 pounds fresh boneless pork butt, trimmed, cut into 1" cubes

2 tablespoons lard

2 onions, sliced thin

1 red bell pepper, sliced thin

2 tomatoes, peeled, seeded and chopped

1/4 teaspoon cayenne

24 little neck clams, scrubbed

1/4 cup chopped fresh coriander

1/4 cup fresh parsley, minced

Preparation

To make Marinated Pork with Clams: Combine the wine, paprika, bay leaf, 1 1/2 teaspoons salt, black pepper and garlic in a stainless steel bowl. Add the pork and mix well to coat evenly. Cover with plastic wrap and marinate for three hours at room temperature. Drain the pork and save the marinade. Discard the bay leaf and pat the pork dry with paper towels.

In a large skillet, heat 1 tablespoon of the lard over moderately high heat until hot, but not smoking. Brown the pork in batches in the hot lard, turning, for 6 to 8 minutes, or until pork is just cooked through. Transfer cooked pork with slotted spoon to another bowl. Add to the skillet the remaining lard, reduce the heat to moderately low and add onions and bell pepper. Cook with stirring until onions are softened. Add reserved marinade, the tomatoes, the remaining teaspoon of salt and the cayenne and simmer covered for 5 minutes. Add the clams and simmer the mixture for an additional 5 minutes or until the clams are opened. Discard any unopened clams. Add the cooked pork and simmer, stirring, for an additional 3 minutes.

Sprinkle with the coriander, parsley and additional black pepper. Add additional salt and pepper to taste. Serve with saffron rice. Serves 4.

Chef's Suggested Menu

~

Carmarao a Guiho
(shrimp in garlic sauce)

Bacalhau Assado a Sacavern
(broiled codfish)

Passarinhos Grelhados
(broiled quail)

Carne de Porco a Alentejana
(marinated pork with clams)

Doce de Queijo
(Iberian cheesecake)

~

Iberia Peninsula

We Welcome
Diners Club International

Il Capriccio

ITALIAN

Lunch Monday – Friday
Dinner Monday – Saturday
Open Sunday for Special Parties

Gentlemen: Jackets & Ties

Valet Parking

Piano Music Monday–Friday

Elegant Wedding &
Corporate Party Facilities

Gourmet 9-Course Dinners
with Wine

Accepts Diners Club and Other
Major Credit Cards

---

633 ROUTE 10 EAST
WHIPPANY, NJ
201.884.9175

Founded in 1984 by chef-owner Antonio Grande and his wife Clara, Il Capriccio is a deluxe restaurant not content to sit on its laurels. Il Capriccio's lavish mauve and burgundy quarters are artfully adorned with elegant decorative touches and exotic floral arrangements. Its cuisine is at the cutting edge of regional Italian cookery; its wine cellar, which includes a large variety of Italian, French and California bottles, is a consistent award winner; and its formally dressed servers are splendid. Il Capriccio has been rated one of New Jersey's top five Northern Italian restaurants by *Zagat Tri-State Restaurant Survey*, won "Best of the Best" poll seven years in a row by *New Jersey Monthly* Readers Poll 1987-1993 and received stellar ratings from *The New York Times* and *The Star-Ledger*.

FILETTO DI BUE AL GORGONZOLA

INGREDIENTS

1/2 pound gorgonzola cheese

4 tablespoons pignolia nuts

4 fresh basil leaves, chopped

A pinch of parsley, chopped

A pinch black pepper

2 ounces parmigiana cheese, grated (about 1/3 cup)

8 4 ounce slices filet mignon (pounded 1/8 inch thick)

8 thin slices of spec (about 2 ounces of Italian smoked prosciutto)

1/4 cup flour

2 tablespoons clarified butter

4 fresh sage leaves

3 ounces dry white wine

1/2 cup beef broth

1/2 cup brown sauce

PREPARATION

Mix gorgonzola cheese with pignolia nuts, basil, parsley, black pepper and parmigiana cheese. Place equal amounts of the mixture in the centers of each filet mignon slice and roll. Wrap each roll with a slice of spec, dust with flour and sauté in a large skillet in clarified butter (very high heat) about 5 minutes or until golden brown. Add the sage and white wine to the skillet. Boil and reduce the liquid for one minute. Add the broth and brown gravy and mix well.

Place the rolled steaks with the sauce in a preheated oven at 450° F for 15 minutes. Serve immediately.

CHEF'S SUGGESTED MENU

Ostriche al Prosecco
(oysters in Prosecco wine sauce)

Papparadelle ai Porcini
(wide housemade pasta with porcini mushrooms)

Costatine D'Agnello ai Tre Pepi
(lamb chops, three pepper sauce)

Filetto di Bue al Gorgonzola con Polenta

Midnight Cake
Chocolate Mousse, Cheesecake

Il Tulipano

ITALIAN

Lunch Tuesday – Friday
Dinner Every Day

Gentlemen: Jackets and Ties

Valet Parking

Piano Music
Tuesday – Saturday

Elegant Party Facilities

Accepts Diners Club and Other
Major Credit Cards

1131 Pompton Avenue
Cedar Grove, NJ
201.256.9300

Il Tulipano genuine renditions of Italian regional cuisine, complemented by a diverse selection of notable wines and distinguished, highly professional service staff, have won rave notices from gastronomes and restaurant reviewers since its inception in 1982. Some of these kudos include: among the top 50 food ratings in the Tri-State area, one of the top two in Northern Italian cuisine, and premier ratings for decor and service in the *Zagat Tri-State Restaurant Survey*. Established by Gregorio Polimeni, one of America's acknowledged pacesetters promoting Italian gastronomy in America, Il Tulipano's cuisine is based on the traditional Italian respect for the finest in fresh ingredients and cooking techniques that showcase natural taste. The unpretentiously chic, warm surroundings create an ideal ambiance for handsomely presented fare mirroring the healthful, classical cookery of Italy. A wide variety of classic pasta preparations and unequivocally fresh seafood are only some of the extra-ordinary Tulipano options. The dessert cart contains seductive delicacies that sway dieters' resolve.

FETTINE MARGHERITA

INGREDIENTS

1 pound San Marzano tomatoes, drained

2 tablespoons extra virgin olive oil

3 leaves of fresh basil, cut in julienne strips

A pinch of fresh thyme

Salt and pepper to taste

12 thin slices of milk fed veal, preferably cut tenderloin (about 1 1/2 pounds)

Flour for dusting the veal

1/4 cup clarified butter

6 cooked small artichoke hearts, cut in half vertically

12 thin slices of mozzarella cheese

24 pitted Gaeta olives

PREPARATION

Place tomatoes in a food processor and jog a few times to dice and blend. Add extra virgin olive oil, basil, thyme, pepper and salt to taste. Mix well and reserve.

Pound veal very thin and lightly dust with flour, shaking off the excess. Heat clarified butter in a skillet over high heat. Sauté veal in batches very lightly on both sides (about 30 seconds each side) and reserve.

Place tomato blend in a skillet or baking pan large enough to fit the veal in a single layer. Place sautéed veal over the tomato blend. Top veal slices with 1/2 an artichoke, a slice of mozzarella cheese and 2 olives. Bake in a preheated oven at 400° F for 10 minutes. Serve immediately. Serves 6.

CHEF'S SUGGESTED MENU

Salmone Affumicato
(freshly smoked salmon classically garnished)

Pappardelle alla Vodka
(homemade pasta strips with fresh tomato essence, young peas, basil and vodka)

Battuta di Pollo alla Griglia
(butterflied breast of chicken marinated in a subtle variety of herbs and spices, then grilled and capped with fresh strips of pepper)

Fettine Margherita

Chocolate Mousse

il Tulipano

We Welcome
Diners Club International

Il Villino

ITALIAN

*Lunch Monday – Friday
Dinner Daily*
Jackets for Dinner
Valet Parking for Dinner
Private Party Facilities
*Accepts Diners Club and Other
Major Credit Cards*

53 FRANKLIN TURNPIKE
WALDWICK, NJ
201.652.8880

IL VILLINO IS A DELUXE RISTORANTE WHERE ADMIRABLE CLASSIC AND MODERN ITALIAN CUISINE IS EXPERTLY INTEGRATED WITH HIGHLY POLISHED GRACIOUS SERVICE AND FINE WINES IN A STATELY SETTING SUGGESTIVE OF A LUXURIOUS VILLA. FOR THE BROTHERS ALESSANDRO AND GEORGIO COLLINI, THIS URBANE RESTAURANT IN THE TINY TOWN OF WALDWICK IS THE REALIZATION OF THEIR LIFE-LONG AMBITION. FOR THEIR PATRONS AND THEIR CRITICS FROM *THE NEW YORK TIMES* AND *THE RECORD*, IL VILLINO IS A GEM WORTHY OF TOP BILLING. THE MENU, WHICH CHANGES WITH THE SEASONS, EMBRACES EPICUREAN DELIGHTS LIKE FRESH TAGLIOLINI TOSSED WITH FRESH TOMATO AND BASIL, DICED SHRIMP, SCALLOPS, LOBSTER AND SALMON ON A VERDANT PARSLEY SAUCE AND A VEAL CHOP ROASTED IN PORT WINE WITH POACHED PEARS AND BRAISED LEEKS. AT IL VILLINO, DINING IS AKIN TO AN EXPERIENCE IN A RENOWNED RISTORANTE IN ITALY, MINUS THE COST OF AIR FARE.

Semi Freddo

Ingredients

4 eggs yolks

6 ounces sugar

1 tablespoon honey

1 tablespoon cognac

7 ounces Torrone candy, finely chopped

1/4 pound Amaretto cookies, finely chopped

2 cups heavy cream, whipped

4 egg whites, beaten stiff

Pistachio Sauce:
8 egg yolks

1/2 cup sugar

2 tablespoons flour

1 1/2 cups milk

1/2 vanilla bean

4 tablespoons pistachio nuts, finely chopped

Preparation

Make the Semi Fredo: Whip egg yolks with sugar until creamy. Whip in honey and cognac. Fold in the Torrone and Amaretto cookies and mix until uniform. Fold in the whipped cream into the mixture. Fold in the egg whites into the mixture. Pour into custard cups, cover with plastic wrap and freeze for 8 to 10 hours (or overnight).

Make the Pistachio Sauce: Whip the egg yolks together with the sugar and flour with wire whisk until creamy. In the top of a double boiler, add the milk and vanilla bean and heat over boiling water until milk is hot. Remove vanilla bean and add hot milk a little at a time to the yolk mixture with constant whisking. When milk and yolk mixture is incorporated, return pot to the top of the double boiler. Cook the mixture with whisking until thick. Place top of double boiler in a pot of ice water with cubes. Continue to whisk until sauce is cold. Pour sauce over the semi fredo, top with chopped pistachio nuts and serve.

Chef's Suggested Menu

Fresh Linguine
Tossed with Diced Fresh Tomato,
Basil, Shrimp, Scallops,
Lobster and Salmon in a
Verdant Parsley Sauce

Chilled Roasted Eggplant Soup
Accented with
Romano Cheese and Basil Scented
Mascarpone Cheese

Mache Field Greens
with Sliced Cucumbers, Fresh Beets,
Crumbled Goat Cheese
and Toasted Walnuts Tossed with a
Lemon/Extra Virgin Olive Oil
Vinaigrette

Seared Sea Scallops with
a Romaine Lettuce Sauce and Frizzled
Mixed Summer Vegetables

Torrone Semi Freddo with
Pistachio Sauce

We Welcome

The Inn at Millrace Pond

~

AMERICAN

Dinner Every Day
Special Sunday Lunch & Dinner
Breakfast for Overnight Guests Only

Proper Attire Please

Self-Parking

Piano Music on Saturdays

Elegant Party & Wedding Facilities
Corporate Conference Facilities

17 Individually Decorated
Guest Rooms

Accepts Diners Club and Other
Major Credit Cards

Route 519
Hope, NJ
908.459.4884

The Inn at Millrace Pond — which reflects the finest colonial traditions of hospitality, gracious service and fine food, spirits and lodging — is ideal for a getaway weekend or a splendid dining experience. ❧ The original Moravian village's impressive grist mill serves as the focal point of the painstakingly restored inn complex — with an exciting tavern and restaurant, plus comfortable accommodations in charming rooms with private baths and modern amenities. ❧ The entire inn is decorated to capture the elegance of Colonial America. ❧ The cuisine changes with the seasons, utilizing superior fresh ingredients in dishes that capture their rich natural tastes. ❧ The *Zagat Tri-State Restaurant Survey* gave this stellar inn some of its highest ratings for food, decor and service.

Roast Breast of Duck
FINISHED WITH A CRANBERRY/CURRANT/GRAND MARNIER DEMI-GLACE

Ingredients

- 3 whole mallard or Long Island duck breasts, center cartilage removed
- Salt and pepper
- 12 ounces fresh cranberries
- 4 ounces currants (scant cup)
- 1 teaspoon orange zest
- 1 teaspoon lemon zest
- 1/2 cup white sugar
- 1/4 cup dry white wine
- 1/4 cup Grand Marnier
- 1/4 cup fresh orange juice
- 1 cup brown game stock

Gingered Rice:
- 2 tablespoon butter
- 1/2 cup leeks (white part only, cut julienne, washed well)
- 1 tablespoon grated fresh ginger
- 3 ounces chicken or veal stock
- 1/4 pound wild rice and brown rice cooked al dente
- Salt and pepper

Preparation

Split breasts in half, score skin side in a diamond pattern and season with salt and pepper. Heat skillet over medium heat, place duck breasts skin-side down and cook, pouring off fat as it accumulates, until skin is crisp (about 4 minutes). Turn and continue to cook until meat is medium rare (1 to 2 minutes additional). Remove duck to platter and keep warm in a preheated oven at 200° F. Add cranberries, currants, zest and sugar to juice in the skillet and cook until the cranberries are soft. Deglaze the skillet with white wine, Grand Marnier and orange juice. Add the brown stock and season with salt and pepper to taste. Slice each duck breast in a fan pattern, place on warmed plates and ladle sauce evenly over all the breasts.

Gingered Rice: Melt butter in a preheated sauce pan over low heat. Add leeks and ginger and cook over low heat (sweat). Deglaze pan with chicken or veal stock and add rice mixture. Toss ingredients lightly while heating. Season with salt and pepper to taste. (Optional: confit of duck leg may be added to rice.) Serves 6.

Chef's Suggested Menu

Warmed Goat Cheese Tart Accented with Mache, Roasted Bell Peppers and Balsamic Vinaigrette

Shrimp Bisque Garnished with Fresh Dill

Roast Breast of Duck Finished with a Cranberry, Currant and Grand Marnier Demi-glace

Fresh Seasonal Berries

The Inn at Millrace Pond

We Welcome
Diners Club International

KEN MARCOTTE

AMERICAN / CONTEMPORARY

*Lunch Monday – Friday
Dinner Every Day*
Jackets Requested
Self-Parking
Elegant Party Facilities
Off Premise Catering
*Accepts Diners Club and Other
Major Credit Cards*

115 ELM STREET
WESTFIELD, NJ
908.233.2309

KEN MARCOTTE, THE OWNER/CHEF OF THE HANDSOME RESTAURANT THAT BEARS HIS NAME, IS PART OF A CADRE OF HOME-GROWN INVENTIVE CHEFS CHANGING THE WORLD'S IMAGE OF AMERICAN GASTRONOMY. HIS CREATIVE COOKERY, SOLIDLY BASED ON CLASSICAL FRENCH-CODIFIED TECHNIQUES, UTILIZES TOP QUALITY SEASONAL INGREDIENTS IN DISHES THAT DAZZLE THE EYES AND TASTE BUDS. LAUDED BY PATRONS AND CRITICS, THIS STYLISH RESTAURANT, WITH A SPLENDID SELECTION OF WINES, WAS LISTED AS ONE OF "NORTHERN NEW JERSEY'S MOST POPULAR RESTAURANTS" AND IN THE TOP FOOD RATINGS IN THE *ZAGAT TRI-STATE RESTAURANT SURVEY*. KEN MARCOTTE WAS ALSO RATED THREE STARS IN "NEW JERSEY'S BEST DINING" BY THE RESTAURANT REVIEWERS OF *THE NEW YORK TIMES*, NEW JERSEY SECTION.

Chocolate Hazelnut Cake

Ingredients

1 pound of semi-sweet chocolate

1/2 cup sweetened praline paste (unsweetened peanut butter may be substituted)

1/4 pound butter, melted (one stick)

1/2 cup heavy cream

1/2 cup hazelnuts, chopped

6 eggs separated

1/3 cup sugar

Preparation

Preheat oven to 350° F. Butter and sugar a 10" spring form pan. Melt chocolate and praline paste in a large bowl placed over a pot of barely simmering water. Remove from the heat and add melted butter and mix well. Add the cream and mix well. Stir in nuts.

Beat egg whites in a large mixer at high speed until soft peaks are formed. Add sugar a little at a time with constant mixing and then add the egg yolks. Continue to beat until mixture is doubled (about 3 minutes). Fold the egg mixture into the chocolate, 1/3 at a time, until it is just incorporated. Do not over fold.

Pour mixture into the spring form pan. Bake in a 350° F preheated oven for 45 to 50 minutes or until it tests done.

Chef's Suggested Menu

Lobster
Over Celery Root Salad Accented
with Chives Gewurtztraminer

Grilled Quail
Over Grilled Leeks with a
Three Mustard Vinaigrette

Grilled Salmon and Foie Gras
Over Green Lentils
with a Cabernet Sauce

Flourless Chocolate Hazelnut Cake
Accented with
White Chocolate Shavings

We Welcome

Knife and Fork Inn

AMERICAN/SEAFOOD

*Lunch & Dinner in the Winter
Tuesday – Saturday*

*Dinner Only in the Summer
Tuesday – Sunday
Closed Mondays All Year*

Jackets for Gentlemen – No Jeans

Self-Parking

Party Facilities

*Accepts Diners Club and Other
Major Credit Cards*

Albany and
Atlantic Avenues
Atlantic City, NJ
609.344.1133

Wise diners who appreciate fine food don't gamble when it comes to selecting a place to dine in Atlantic City. That's why the sophisticated Atlantic City crowd chooses the Knife and Fork Inn for lunch and dinner. This charming, urbane establishment treats patrons to splendid food, with an emphasis on expertly prepared, unequivocally fresh seafood, complemented by fine wines and proficiently served by a professional wait-staff. For more than 65 years a legion of cosmopolitan regulars accustomed to the world's finest cuisine have been beating a path to the Knife and Fork's door. And, they have been consistently rewarded with an excellent dining experience by three generations of the Latz family. Currently, Mack Latz and his son, Andrew, carry on the tradition that has won oodles of stars and accolades from restaurant critics and diners alike.

Knife & Fork Bouillabaisse

Ingredients

- 3 tablespoons olive oil
- 1 cup onions, minced (1 medium)
- 1/2 cup leeks, white part diced (1 medium)
- 4 pounds of ripe fresh tomatoes, peeled, seeded and coarsely chopped
- 5 large garlic cloves
- 2 cups dry white wine
- 2 1/2 cups chicken broth
- 6 drops of Tabasco
- 1 teaspoon paprika
- 3 teaspoons fennel seeds, crushed
- 1/4 cup bouquet garni (a mixture of fresh thyme, savory, basil, oregano; 1 tablespoon each, chopped fine)
- 1" piece of dried orange peel
- Pinch of saffron
- Salt to taste (1 3/4 teaspoons)
- Pepper to taste (1/2 teaspoon)
- 1/4 to 1 pound live lobster, cut into bite sized pieces
- 1 pound of mussels, scrubbed and clean
- 1/2 pound of shrimp, peeled and deveined
- 1 pound of flounder, cut into 2" pieces
- 1 pound red snapper, cut into 2" pieces

Preparation

In large heavy bottom non-reactive soup pot, heat the olive oil over medium low heat. Add the onions and leeks and cook with occasional stirring with a wooden spoon until the vegetables are softened without becoming brown (about 6 to 7 minutes). Add the chopped tomatoes and garlic, cover and simmer for 10 minutes. Remove from the heat and place the mixture in a food processor. Jog for only 3 minutes to blend (do not pureé). Return the blend to the pot, add wine and bring to a very low boil for about 3 minutes.

Add chicken broth, Tabasco, paprika, fennel seeds, bouquet garni, orange peel and saffron. Simmer for 35 minutes, uncovered allowing sauce to reduce. Add salt (about 1 3/4 teaspoons) and pepper (about 1/2 teaspoon) to taste. Add the prepared lobster first, cook for 2 minutes, add mussels, cook another 2 minutes, add the shrimp, the flounder and the snapper and cook for 3 minutes longer. Serve with sliced French bread rubbed with garlic.

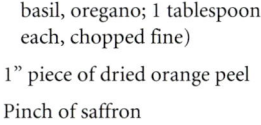

Chef's Suggested Menu

Smoked Tuna
Horseradish Sauce

Mussels Mariniere

Knife & Fork Seafood Bouillabaisse

Watercress Salad

Cheesecake with Seasonal Berries

We Welcome

LA CUCINA
RISTORANTE & CAFE

ITALIAN

Lunch Monday – Friday
Dinner Every Day
Seasonal Outdoor Dining in its Cafe

Self-Parking

Elegant Party Facilities

Off Premise Catering

Accepts Diners Club and Other
Major Credit Cards

125 WEST MAIN STREET
SOMERVILLE, NJ
908.526.4907

*L*A CUCINA RISTORANTE & CAFE IS A VERY HANDSOME DINING SPOT WITH SUPERIOR RENDITIONS OF THE REGIONAL CUISINE OF ITALY MATCHED WITH AN EXTENSIVE SELECTION OF WINES AND EXCEPTIONAL SERVICE. NOT SURPRISING, IT CONSISTENTLY WINS PRAISES FROM ITS CLIENTELE AND THE APPLAUSE OF THE CRITICS. IT WAS FREQUENTLY VOTED "BEST OF THE BEST" AND CITED IN 1993 AS "BEST ITALIAN" IN *NEW JERSEY MONTHLY'S* READERS' CHOICE AWARDS. *NEW JERSEY MONTHLY* RESTAURANT CRITICS ALSO RATED LA CUCINA THREE AND A HALF STARS AND IT WAS MERITED "VERY GOOD" BY THE RESTAURANT REVIEWERS OF *THE NEW YORK TIMES*, NEW JERSEY SECTION. THIS CHIC, BI-LEVEL MEDITERRANEAN-STYLE RESTAURANT ALSO OFFERS AL FRESCO DINING IN ITS SEASONAL OUTDOOR CAFE AND INTIMATE GOURMET DINNERS IN ITS PRIVATE WINE CELLAR DINING ROOM.

Ravioli alla Ortalana

Ingredients

- 1 garlic clove, sliced
- 2 tablespoons extra virgin olive oil
- 4 tablespoons zucchini, finely diced
- 4 tablespoons yellow squash, finely diced
- 3 1/2 tablespoons turnips, finely diced
- 3 tablespoons carrots, finely diced
- 3 tablespoons red onion, finely diced
- 3 tablespoons plum tomatoes, finely diced
- 6 ounces chicken stock
- 1 pinch kosher salt
- 1 pinch black pepper
- 1 pinch sugar
- 1 teaspoon butter
- 16 to 20 spinach & cheese ravioli (fresh market available cheese ravioli may be substituted)
- 1/4 cup freshly grated parmigiana reggiano cheese (more or less to taste)

Preparation

In a skillet, brown the garlic in olive oil. Add the diced vegetables and sauté for 1 minute. Add the stock and seasonings. Bring to a boil over high heat and cook 3 to 4 minutes until reduced. Add the butter and whisk to thicken.

Cook ravioli in a large pot of boiling salted water until done. Drain well and combine them with the vegetable sauce. Top the ravioli with the grated cheese and serve immediately.

Chef's Suggested Menu

Funghi Misti
(exotic mushrooms sautéed with garlic and balsamic vinegar, over a bed of arugula)

Ravioli alla Ortalana

Tonno alla Griglia
(grilled tuna with a puttanesca salsa and sautéed spinach)

Manzo Tutto Pepe
(filet mignon with cracked black pepper, mushroom reduction)

Almond Semi-Fredo

L'Affaire 22

FRENCH

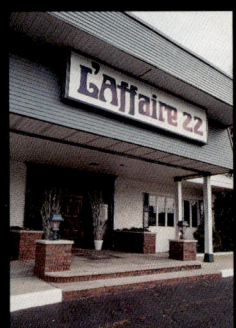

Lunch Monday – Friday
Dinner Every Day

Early Dining Special
Daily 4:30 – 6:00 pm
Sunday 12:30 – 5:00 pm

Country Club Casual Attire

Self-Parking

Elegant Party Facilities

Off Premise Catering

Accepts Diners Club and Other
Major Credit Cards

1099 Route 22 East
Mountainside, NJ
908.232.4454

Diners have been having a continuous love affair with L'Affaire 22 and the solidly satisfying creative cuisine of chef/restaurateur Robert Connelly for more than a couple of decades. Mr. Connelly, who graduated from the renowned Culinary Institute of America in 1963 and rose to the top of his profession at New York's finest restaurants, introduced New Jersey residents to creative American fare with a classic French touch. Recognizing his significant contributions to the industry, Mr. Connelly was voted "Restaurateur of the Year" in 1992 by the New Jersey Restaurant Association. His signature dishes have been copied by many, but rarely cloned. Chef Connelly also pioneered the introduction of his "Healthy Heart" menu at L'Affaire 22 to provide patrons with delectable dishes that don't abuse their health. For a culinary affair to remember or a healthful business lunch or dinner, L'Affaire is the place.

Sirloin Steak au Poivre

Ingredients

1/3 cup peppercorns, crushed

4 shell steaks, well trimmed (about 10 to 12 ounces each)

2 tablespoons clarified butter (vegetable oil optional)

2 ounces of brandy

1/2 cup beef stock

1 cup heavy cream

2 teaspoons fresh chives, chopped

Salt to taste

Preparation

Spread the crushed peppercorns evenly on a flat surface. Place the steak on the peppercorns and press firmly to coat. Repeat the process on both sides of all the steaks. Heat the clarified butter in a very large skillet over medium high heat. Cook the steaks on both sides (about 6 minutes total for rare, 10 minutes for medium). Remove and reserve on warm platter.

Remove the skillet from the heat and add the brandy. Carefully return the skillet to the stove (the brandy will probably flame if you are using a gas range). Cook the brandy over medium heat for 30 seconds and add stock. Boil until the mixture is reduced by half. Add the cream and the juices from the reserved steaks and simmer for 4 to 5 minutes over medium heat. Add chives and salt to taste and mix well. Add the steaks back to the skillet and cook for 1 minute. Remove the steaks to serving plates and pour the sauce evenly over the steaks. Serve immediately. Serves 4.

Chef's Suggested Menu

Crab Cake Delmonico
(Maryland crab meat sautéed, mustard mayonnaise dressing)

L'Affaire Special Mixed Appetizer
(coconut shrimp, stuffed mushrooms, shrimp nicoise and a crepe of seafood, each with a unique sauce)

Lobster in Whisky
(lobster tail sautéed, whisky flambe, herbs and cream finished and served over a bed of rice pilaf)

Sirloin Steak au Poivre

L'Affaire 22 Coupe
(vanilla ice cream topped with sliced strawberries bathed with a vanilla brandy sauce and topped with whipped cream)

We Welcome

La Gondola

ITALIAN

Lunch Monday – Friday
Dinner Monday – Saturday
Closed Sundays

Proper Attire

Self-Parking

Elegant Party Facilities

*Gourmet Private Parties
in a Rustic Wine Cellar Setting*

*Accepts Diners Club and Other
Major Credit Cards*

762 Roebling Avenue
Trenton, NJ
609.392.0600

La Gondola, a charming, attractive Mediterranean-style ristorante in the historic Chambersburg restaurant district of Trenton, is one of only eight New Jersey restaurants selected to be a member of the prestigious "Gruppo Ristoratori Italiani" — an organization of more than one hundred serious Italian restaurants in America that is dedicated to presenting the "true taste of Italy." La Gondola's authentic cucina Italiana and skilled, unpretentious service earned it an enviable reputation with a legion of loyal patrons and oodles of stars from the restaurant critics. Its extensive wine selection, well matched to complement the food, has been accorded "The Wine Spectator's Award of Excellence". Distinctive, authentic specialties at La Gondola include delectable homemade pasta like Pappardelle al Prosciutto (wide noodles with imported prosciutto from Parma) and other delicacies too numerous to mention.

FILETTO DI VITELLO AL TARTUFO NERO

INGREDIENTS

- 6 tablespoons olive oil
- 2 pounds trimmed milk-fed veal tenderloins, cut cross wise into 1/4" thick slices
- 1/2 cup all-purpose unbleached flour
- 1 garlic clove, diced
- 4 ounces whole black truffles (fresh or canned) sliced thin
- 1 cup heavy cream
- 1/2 cup freshly grated parmigiana reggiano cheese
- 2 tablespoons fresh parsley, minced

PREPARATION

In a heavy skillet, heat the oil over high heat. Dust the veal in the flour, shaking off excess. Add the garlic and the veal to the pan and sauté the meat, in batches, for 3 to 4 minutes or until it is lightly brown on both sides. Add the truffles (and 4 tablespoons of truffle liquid if canned) and simmer the mixture for 2 minutes. Transfer the veal with a slotted spoon to a warm platter.

Add the cream to the skillet and boil it for 1 minute. Whisk in the cheese. Return veal and any juices from the platter to the skillet and coat the veal with the sauce. Sprinkle the veal with the parsley and serve it with baby asparagus (cooked al dente). Serves 6.

CHEF'S SUGGESTED MENU

Pappardelle al Prosciutto
(wide homemade pasta tossed with sautéed onions, parma ham and parmesan cheese)

Filetto di Vitello al Tartufo Nero

Grigliata Mista
(mixed grill of lamb chops, veal chops and quail)

Tiramisu

Lahiere's

F R E N C H / C O N T E M P O R A R Y

*Open for Lunch & Dinner
Monday – Saturday
Closed Sundays*

Jackets Preferred for Dinner

Self-Parking

Elegant Party Facilities

*Accepts Diners Club and Other
Major Credit Cards*

5-11 WITHERSPOON STREET
PRINCETON, NJ
609.921.2798

The legendary Lahiere's, a Princeton gastronomic tradition where guests like Albert Einstein have dined, has been winning kudos since 1919. With the addition of its chef Scott Sueskind (fresh from stints as Sous Chef to Craig Shelton at the Ryland Inn and previously at Dennis Foy's Townsquare) to its polished service staff and encyclopedic selection of wines, Lahiere's will continue to be a haven for central New Jersey gastronomes. Last year Lahiere's was honored for the ninth time with the *Wine Spectator* "Grand Award" (its highest award given to restaurants "where dedication to fine dining and a passion for wine resulted in "a world-class wine list"). In addition *New Jersey Monthly* Reader's Choice Awards listed Lahiere's as Central New Jersey's "Best French" restaurant. Savants of sophisticated dining go out of their way for a memorable experience at Lahiere's

Rack of Lamb with Bayaldi

Ingredients

For the Bayaldi:
1 1/2 tablespoons pommace olive oil (or pure olive oil)

2 cups Spanish onions, peeled and sliced very thin

Salt and fresh ground black pepper to taste

1 medium eggplant, peeled, cut crosswise in 1/4" slices

2 zucchini, cut crosswise in 1/4" slices

2 beefsteak tomatoes, cut crosswise in 1/4" slices (use stem scraps for sauce)

5 sprigs thyme, leaves removed, stems discarded

3 tablespoon of olive oil

For the rack of lamb:
1 full rack of lamb (16 bones)

1 carrot coarsely chopped (about 1/2 cup)

1 cup Spanish onions, coarsely chopped

2 celery ribs, coarsely chopped (about 1/2 cup)

2 garlic cloves, peeled and crushed (2 tablespoons)

1 1/2 tablespoon pommace olive oil

5 sprigs of thyme

2 1/2 cups lamb stock (or brown stock)

4 sprigs parsley

Preparation

For the Bayaldi: To a saute pan over low heat add olive oil, onions, salt and pepper. Cook slowly over low heat for 30 minutes to confit texture and put into a 9" square baking dish. Laminate slices of eggplant with zucchini and tomatoes, place the laminates over the onion mixture in a shingle-like pattern. Sprinkle the top with thyme leaves and drizzle with extra virgin olive oil plus additional salt and pepper to taste. Cover and bake in a preheated oven at 300° F for 40 minutes. Uncover and bake an additional 15 minutes. Remove from the oven.

For the lamb: Have the butcher "french" the rack, cutting the bones in small pieces and giving them to you with the meat scraps. To a roasting pan add lamb bones and meat scraps, carrots, onions, celery and garlic and roast in a preheated oven at 400° F for 10 minutes. Season rack of lamb with pommace oil and sear in a large skillet over high heat. Press thyme sprigs on the meat, place rack of lamb on browned bone mixture and roast in a preheated oven at 400° F, basting frequently, for about 20 minutes (for medium rare). Remove lamb from the oven and keep warm in a preheated oven at 200° F. Pour off fat from the roasting pan and deglaze with stock over medium high heat, scraping the browned bits. Add parsley and tomato stem scraps and barely simmer for 10 minutes. Strain through a sieve into a sauce pan.

Assembly: Cut Bayaldi into 4 sections and place them in the center of preheated plates. Cut lamb into single chops and arrange on the plate, bones inward, around the Bayaldi. Nape with the sauce. Serve with mashed potatoes. Serves 4.

Chef's Suggested Menu

Warm Salad
of Wild Mushrooms and Frissee

Mushroom Vinaigrette Vegetable
Soup with Beans and Pistou

Red Snapper with Spinach
and Chive Potatoes, Lobster Jus

Rack of Lamb with Bayaldi

Gratin of Seasonal Fruit

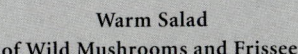

Lahiere's
Since 1919

L'Allegria

ITALIAN

Lunch Monday – Friday
Dinner Monday – Saturday
Closed Sundays

Proper Attire Please

Self-Parking

Elegant Party Facilities

Accepts Diners Club and Other
Major Credit Cards

9-11 Prospect Street
Madison, NJ
201.377.6808

L'Allegria, conceived by brothers Saverio and Giovanni Allocca in 1984, experienced a meteoric rise to stardom. It has maintained its lofty status due to the Allocca's dedication to optimum quality. The fashionable ristorante, with the casual feel of al fresco dining in a Mediterranean courtyard, features proficient, unpretentious European-style service, a distinguished wine cellar and a kitchen staff led by the renowned Master Chef, Donato Deserio, known in New York City as the capo di cucina. The delicate blend of exquisite renditions of authentic cuisine and wines from Italy's diverse regions, coupled with L'Allegria's charming ambiance, create the quintessential Italian dining experience. As a result, L'Allegria consistently wins the acclaim of restaurant critics and the applause of diners.

SALMONE FARCITO CON ZUCCHINI ALLA MENTA

Ingredients

- 8 garlic cloves, peeled
- 6 tablespoons extra virgin olive oil
- 1 pound zucchini, cut in wedges
- Salt and pepper
- 1/4 cup balsamic vinegar
- 34 mint leaves
- 2 pounds fresh salmon fillets (3" x 1/4" sticks)

Preparation

In a skillet, over medium heat, sauté 4 cloves of garlic in 2 tablespoons of olive oil until golden brown. Add zucchini and cook with constant stirring for 2 to 3 minutes (al dente). Remove from the skillet and place in a bowl. Add salt and pepper to taste. Cool to room temperature and add 2 tablespoons of balsamic vinegar and 24 mint leaves. Pour 2 tablespoons oil and 1 tablespoon of balsamic vinegar in a baking pan with 4 garlic cloves and 10 more mint leaves.

Cut salmon diagonally, flipping over each slice (1/4" thick) towards the tail. Place the salmon in the baking pan. Add the zucchini (2 wedges at a time) and 2 mint leaves, 2 wedges at a time, between the salmon slices, flipping the salmon, over towards the opposite direction. Top with the rest of the ingredients and let it marinate for about 2 hours. Place baking pan with the salmon in a preheated oven at 500° F and bake for 10 minutes. Serve immediately. Serves 6.

Chef's Suggested Menu

Prati e Scogli
(a combination of grilled smoked mozzarella cheese, shellfish, portobello mushrooms and diced fresh tomatoes)

Striscette di Granito Vegetale al Suga di Quaglie con Rosmarino
(multi-colored pasta ribbons tinted with arugula, radicchio and carrots, tossed with a quail-enriched sauce)

Salmon Farcito con Zucchini alla Menta
(salmon marinated with extra virgin olive oil and balsamic vinegar, stuffed with sautéed zucchini and mint and roasted)

Scorzette di Manzo con Pan Tostato
(grilled marinated sliced beef served on garlic toast)

Sorbetto Limone con Lampone
(lemon sorbet garnished with raspberries)

We Welcome

Lantana

ITALIAN

Lunch Tuesday – Friday
Dinner Tuesday – Sunday

Valet Parking

Private, Social, or Business
Party Facilities

Limousine Service to NY Theaters
and Meadowland Events

Accepts Diners Club and Other
Major Credit Cards

1148 Paterson
Plank Road
Secaucus, NJ
201.867.1065

Lantana was conceived by Frank Vecchiotti, the restaurateur who originated the illustrious Sonny D's on the same site. Sonny's was a glamorous, glitzy '80's dining spot; Lantana is a smart cosmopolitan restaurant pleasing the passion of '90's diners for top-value, sophisticated light cuisine, proficiently served in a fashionable, relaxed setting. True to the traditions of genuine Northern Italian cookery, Lantana's kitchen turns out intensely flavorful, wholesome dishes that emphasize the natural goodness of prime ingredients. Abundant pasta options, like half-moon broccoli-cheese dumplings in a delicate, fresh tomato sauce, are uniformly glorious. Chicken is notably juicy and truly flavorful, fish is prepared in numerous ways that don't upstage their unequivocal fresh, delicate taste and the meats, like a rack of lamb on a savory roasted red pepper purée, are marvelous. Its extensive wine options and solidly satisfying desserts are ideal complements to prudently priced gourmet dining at Lantana.

Roast Loin of Veal with Sweetbread Mousse

Ingredients

For the sweetbread mousse:
1 medium sweetbread (membrane removed)
3 dried morels, soaked, washed and dried (1/3 cup)

For the loin of veal:
3 pound eye loin of veal
2 teaspoons Kosher salt
1/2 teaspoon ground white pepper
8 large spinach leaves, washed and dried (1 cup)

1/2 cup celery, coarsely chopped (2 stalks)
2 cloves garlic, crushed (1 tablespoon)
2 shallots, finely chopped (2 tablespoons)

For the sauce:
4 cups veal or chicken stock
1 teaspoon unsalted butter
1 shallot, finely chopped (1 tablespoon)
1/4 cup heavy cream

Preparation

Sweetbread mousse: In a food processor pureé the sweetbread with the morels.

Preparation of the veal roast: Split the loin of veal lengthwise without cutting it all the way through (butterfly cut). Open the veal, lay flat and season with the salt and pepper. Lay 4 of the spinach leaves in the center of the loin. Spread the sweetbread mousse over the spinach. Place the rest of the spinach over the mousse. Bring the veal back together and tie with kitchen twine. Place the veal in a roasting pan with the celery, garlic and shallots. Roast in a preheated oven at 450° until the veal is done (about 30 minutes). Remove the roast, tent with aluminum foil to keep warm and reserve.

For the sauce: Place liquid and vegetables from the roasting pan in a saucepan with the stock. Boil over high heat until the liquid is reduced to 2 cups (about 20 minutes). Strain the sauce and reserve. Melt the butter in a heavy saucepan over medium heat. Sauté shallots until they are soft (5 minutes) and add the cream. Cook with frequent stirring until the cream in reduced (7 to 8 minutes) and thick enough to coat a spoon. Add the reserved sauce from the veal roast, slowly, stirring to keep the mixture smooth.

To assemble: Cut the veal roast in 1/2 inch slices and spoon sauce over the slices. Serves 10.

Chef's Suggested Menu

Shrimp and Cannellini Beans
(marinated with red onions and herbs)

Tortelli Mezzaluna
(half-moon shaped pasta dumplings filled with ricotta and broccoli tossed with a garlicky oil sauce accented with fresh tomatoes fillets)

Fresh Mixed Seasonal Greens Tossed with a Balsamic Vinaigrette

Roast Loin of Veal with a Sweetbread Mousse

Hazelnut Semi-Fredo With Gianduia Chocolate Sauce

Lantana restaurant

We Welcome

Le Papillon

FRENCH

Lunch Monday – Friday
Dinner Every Day

Gentlemen: Jackets Please

Self-Parking

Elegant Party Facilities

Off Premise Catering

Accepts Diners Club and Other
Major Credit Cards

142 South Street
Morristown, NJ
201.539.8088

Le Papillon is a very cozy storefront restaurant with the look of a French country inn. In this setting owner/maitre d' Terry Nahavandi and his regiment of highly skilled, unpretentious professionals serve thoroughly satisfying, handsomely presented classic and contemporary French dishes that are intelligently matched with a substantial selection of quality French and American wines. Le Papillon specializes in provincial French cuisine that has been labeled "magnifique". Its kudos include a two star rating in "New Jersey's Best Dining" from the restaurant reviews of the New York Times New Jersey Section. Le Papillon is noted among the business and private community for its off premise catering and large, private meeting and party facilities. Dine on tantalizing steak tartare, roast rack of lamb and impeccable fresh fish with delightfully subtle sauces. Souffles are textbook-perfect and splendid finales to a top-value dinner at Papillon.

Rillettes le Papillon

Ingredients

- 2 pounds fatback pork, diced finely (3 cups)
- 1 1/2 pounds fresh lean pork, from the belly, diced finely (2 cups)
- 1 1/2 teaspoons salt
- A dash of pepper to taste
- A pinch of poultry seasoning (1/8 teaspoon)
- 1 bay leaf
- 1 cup boiling water

Preparation

Rillettes is a renown French culinary delicacy resembling a silky smooth pâté. Spread cold on toast or thin slices of a crusty baguette, it's a delightful prelude course and aperitif accompaniment to arouse appetites.

In a heavy pot, combine the fatback, lean pork, salt, pepper, poultry seasoning, bay leaf and boiling water. Simmer the mixture over low heat, stirring occasionally until the water is almost cooked away (about 30 minutes). Raise heat to medium and brown the meat and the fat. Drain the mixture in a colander, saving the fat that drains. Discard the bay leaf and grind the meat very finely. Gradually stir into the mixture all (about 2/3 cup) but 1 cup of the hot fat. Pack the blend into small jars and pour a layer of the hot fat over the meat to cover. Store jars of rillettes in the refrigerator. Serve cold.

Chef's Suggested Menu

Poached Oysters in Champagne Sauce
Over Puff Pastry

Consomme Henry IV

Melange of Lobster and Sea Scallops
in a Saffron Sauce

Baby Rack of Lamb Roasted
with Dijon Mustard and Rosemary

Salad of Endive and Watercress
with Goat Cheese and
a Mustard Vinaigrette

Fresh Fruit Tart,
Filled With Honey Custard

LLEWELLYN FARMS

AMERICAN/CONTINENTAL

Lunch Tuesday – Friday
Dinner Tuesday – Sunday
Sunday Light Dinner Available
in the Early Afternoon

Country Club Casual

Valet Parking

Piano Music Weekends

Elegant Party Facilities

Early Bird Dinner

Accepts Diners Club and Other
Major Credit Cards

ROUTES 202 & 10
MORRIS PLAINS, NJ
201.538.4323

LLEWELLYN FARMS, A LANDMARK ON THE CORNER OF ROUTES 202 AND 10 FOR MORE THAN 50 YEARS, IS A TIMELESS GEM THAT CONSISTENTLY DELIVERS TOP QUALITY FARE IN AN ATTRACTIVE SETTING COUPLED WITH A SUPERB SELECTION OF SENSIBLY-PRICED WINES PLUS FRIENDLY, CAPABLE SERVICE — ALL AT PRICES THAT ARE HARD TO DUPLICATE. LLEWELLYN'S CUISINE IS SIMPLE, OLD FASHIONED AMERICAN/CONTINENTAL FOOD. THAT MEANS THE FARE SERVED PRIMARILY CONSISTS OF THICK CUTS OF ROAST PRIME RIBS OF BEEF, JUICY WELL-AGED STEAKS, DOUBLE-CUT LAMB CHOPS WITH MINT JELLY AND NEW ENGLAND SCROD. OYSTERS ROCKEFELLER, CLAMS CASINO AND ROAST DUCK WITH ORANGE OR CHERRY SAUCE ARE ALSO FAVORITES AMONG THE ARMY OF REGULARS THAT HAS BEEN DINING AT LLEWELLYN FARMS FOR A COUPLE OF GENERATIONS.

Baked Stuffed Prawns Llewellyn

Ingredients

- 5 jumbo prawns (Panama white U-10)
- 4 tablespoons sweet butter
- 2 shallots, minced
- 4 ounces King crabmeat, minced
- 1/2 cup unsalted cracker crumbs
- Salt and pepper
- 2 tablespoon fresh parsley, minced
- 1 teaspoon dry sherry
- 1 tablespoon bacon drippings, from 2 strips of bacon
- 1/4 tablespoon onions, minced
- 1/2 cup chopped spinach, cooked and squeezed dry
- 1 tablespoon heavy cream
- Salt, pepper and nutmeg
- 1 slice American cheese

Preparation

Cut into strips fried onion rings (optional garnish). Peel shrimp and split lengthwise half-way through (or butterflied). Melt butter in skillet over medium heat. Add the shallots and cook until tender (3 to 4 minutes). Add the crabmeat and cook over high heat with constant mixing for 3 minutes. Remove from heat, add the cracker crumbs, salt and pepper to taste and then add the parsley. Add the sherry and mix well to completely incorporate. Reserve.

Heat the bacon drippings in a sauté pan over medium heat and add the minced onions. Sauté until translucent. Add the spinach and cook with mixing until hot. Add the cream, stir and remove from heat. Add salt, pepper and nutmeg to taste. Reserve. Insert 1/5 of the crabmeat blend into each shrimp. Top with 1/5 of the spinach blend. Place American cheese in criss-cross strips over the stuffed shrimp. Place stuffed in buttered casserole and bake in preheated oven at 350°F for 10 to 15 minutes. Serve immediately garnished with onion rings.

Chef's Suggested Menu

~

Perona Farms Smoked Salmon and Smoked Trout, Garnished with Capers and Red Onions; Dill Cream Sauce

Vichyssoise

Baked Stuffed Prawns Llewellyn

Roast Duckling, Brandied Bing Cherry Sauce

Rice Pudding à L'Anglaise

~

THE MANOR

AMERICAN/CONTINENTAL

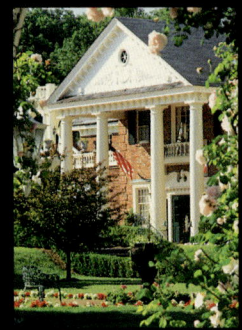

Closed Mondays & Christmas Eve

Gentlemen: Jackets and Ties

Valet & Self-Parking

*Nightly Piano Music: Terrace Lounge
Live Band & Dancing in Le Dôme
Friday and Saturday Evenings*

Elegant Party Facilities

*Chef's Tables, Seafood Festival Buffet
Sunday Candlelight Buffet
Wednesday Lunch Buffet
Express Luncheon Available*

*Accepts Diners Club and Other
Major Credit Cards*

111 PROSPECT AVENUE
WEST ORANGE, NJ
201.731.2360

A GRACIOUS MANOR HOUSE, SET IN ACRES OF MAGNIFICENT FORMAL GARDENS, COMBINES DISTINCTIVE GOURMET CUISINE, SUPERB SERVICE AND ELEGANT DECOR. IN ITS 36 YEARS OF FINE DINING, THE MANOR HAS CONSISTENTLY RECEIVED MANY COVETED AWARDS, AMONG THEM THE DIRŌNA, WHICH PLACES THEM IN THE TOP ONE PERCENT OF NORTH AMERICAN RESTAURANTS. THE RECIPE FOR FINE DINING ALSO INCLUDES THE FOLLOWING AWARDS: MOBIL FOUR STARS, AAA FOUR DIAMONDS, CARTIER'S GOLDEN PLATE FOR ELEGANCE IN DINING, BUSINESS EXECUTIVES DINING AWARD, *THE WINE SPECTATOR* GRAND AWARD, CHEFS 2000 AND THE PRESIDENTIAL INAUGURAL'S "TASTE OF AMERICA." ONE OF THE WORLD'S GREAT LANDMARK RESTAURANTS, THE MANOR HAS BEEN CALLED A "CULINARY VERSAILLES," THE EUROPEAN EXPERIENCE IN AMERICA... WHERE CLASSICAL IS ALWAYS NEW.

Scallops

STUFFED WITH LOBSTER MOUSSE, CHAMPAGNE SAUCE

Ingredients

For the champagne sauce:
1/2 tablespoons shallots, minced
1/2 cup white wine
2 cups fish velouté
1/2 cup champagne
Salt and white pepper to taste
1/3 cup heavy cream

For the scallops:
1/2 teaspoon shallots, minced
1 ounce mushrooms, diced
2 tablespoons sweet butter
6 ounces cooked lobster meat
Whites of 4 large eggs
Salt and white pepper to taste
3/4 cup heavy cream
1/2 teaspoon chives, cut finely
20 large sea scallops, washed well and dried
1/2 cup flour
4 tablespoons butter
2 tablespoons vegetable oil

Preparation

Make the Champagne Sauce: Cook the shallots in a sauce pan with the white wine over medium heat. Boil to reduce to almost dry state. Add veloute and champagne and boil, stirring occasionally, to reduce by 1/2 (about 5 to 7 minutes). Season with salt and pepper. Add cream, strain and serve with scallops.

Make the scallops: Sauté the shallots and mushrooms in butter over low heat for 3 minutes. Set aside to cool. Pureé the lobster meat in a food processor until smooth. Add shallots, mushrooms and egg whites with salt and pepper and pureé until very smooth. Remove from the processor bowl and place in a round mixing bowl. Fold in the heavy cream and chives.

Place lobster mousse in a pastry bag. Split scallops, creating a pocket in the center, and fill with the mousse pushing it into the pocket with the aid of your finger. Gently coat scallops with flour. Melt butter in vegetable oil over low heat. Pan fry the scallops in batches in 2 tablespoons butter/vegetable oil mixture (cleaning the skillet and using fresh butter/oil mixtures between batches). Serve with champagne sauce. Serves 4.

Chef's Suggested Menu

Scallops Stuffed with
Lobster Mousse, Champagne Sauce

Sesame Seared Quail on
a Bed of Greens,
Warm Citrus Vinaigrette

Grilled Fillet of Salmon Trout,
Conundrum Beurre Blanc

Rack of Lamb

Manor Florentines
and Fresh Berries

We Welcome

Mattar's

Italian

Lunch Monday – Friday
Dinner Every Day

Proper Attire Please

Self-Parking

Piano Music Weekends

Elegant Party & Wedding Facilities

Corporate Conference Facilities

Off Premise Catering

Accepts Diners Club and Other
Major Credit Cards

Route 517 & Ridge Road
Allamuchy, NJ
908.852.2300

It was only nine years ago when the Mattar brothers converted a nondescript roadside restaurant into an Italian ristorante with some of the finest food in western New Jersey. Stellar reviews from critics and patrons alike soon followed. But, the physical attributes of the original facility didn't match the sophistication of Mattar's food, wine or formal service. So the Mattars renovated and enlarged the original structure, thereby creating a chic, upscale restaurant that is a beacon of fine dining in rural Allamuchy township, minutes from Interstate 80 and Hackettstown. The captivating atmosphere of Mattar's now matches its excellent creative and classic Italian fare that is complemented by an extensive, judicious selection of wines and an extremely professional, unpretentious staff.

Chicken Giovanni

Ingredients

- All-purpose flour for dusting
- 2 skinless and boneless chicken breasts, tenderloin removed and used for another dish (about 3/4 lb.)
- 4 tablespoons olive oil
- 1 teaspoon minced garlic
- 1/2 cup chicken stock
- 4 tablespoons balsamic vinegar
- 1/2 teaspoon dried oregano
- 2 tablespoons grated fresh romano cheese
- 1 teaspoon of butter
- Salt and pepper

Preparation

Lightly flour the chicken breast. Heat the olive oil in skillet over medium high heat until hot. Sauté the chicken breast, 2 to 3 minutes per side, until it is lightly browned on both sides. Add the garlic and sauté until it lightly browns (about 10 seconds). Add the chicken stock and balsamic vinegar and boil sauce to reduce by 1/3. Add the oregano and romano cheese and mix well. Simmer for a couple of minutes and then swirl in the butter.

Place the chicken on warm plate. Add salt and pepper to taste. Pour the sauce over the chicken and serve immediately. Serves 2.

Chef's Suggested Menu

Calamari Fritto
(golden fried tender squid morsels with a rousing tomato sauce dip)

Tortellini Bolognese
(homemade meat-filled tortellini, sautéed onions, minced prosciutto and peas, bathed with a cream-enriched tomato sauce)

Chicken Giovanni

Filetto Vino Rosso
(twin medallions of filet mignon, topped with mushroom caps, finished with a rich burgundy sauce)

Key Lime Pie

Old Mill Inn

AMERICAN/CONTINENTAL

Lunch Monday – Saturday
Dinner Every Day
Sunday Brunch
Closed Mondays during
the Winter Months
Early Bird Dinner

Casual Dress

Valet and/or Self-Parking

Nightly Piano Music

Elegant Party Facilities

Accepts Diners Club and Other
Major Credit Cards

Old Mill Road
Spring Lake Heights, NJ
908.449.1800

The Old Mill Inn, a New Jersey landmark for more than a half-century, has a clear claim as one of the shore's foremost restaurants. It is truly one of a kind with its wall of windows, which allows diners to enjoy panoramic lakeside views while feasting on superb dry-aged steaks, succulent lobsters and crabs, impeccably fresh fish and standout dishes too numerous to list. The service is provided by a staff of expertly trained servers, and the wine cellar is stocked with an abundant selection of economical and aristocratic bottles that match the cuisine. Winner of the *Asbury Park Press* People's Choice Awards for "Best Overall Restaurant" and "Best Restaurant for Romance," the Old Mill Inn is ideal for business luncheons or dinners, as well as the perfect choice for wedding receptions, private parties and corporate affairs.

CRABCAKES

INGREDIENTS

- 1/4 cup minced yellow onions
- 4 tablespoons melted sweet butter
- 1/4 cup minced green peppers (about 1/2 medium pepper)
- 1/4 cup minced red peppers (about 1/2 medium pepper)
- 2 egg whites
- 6 tablespoons heavy cream
- 2 tablespoons mayonnaise
- 2 tablespoons dijon mustard
- 1 tablespoon Worcestershire sauce
- Dash of Tabasco
- 1 pound Maryland jumbo lump crabmeat, picked over (1/4 cup plus)
- 2 tablespoons unseasoned fresh bread crumbs
- Salt and pepper
- 3/4 cup all purpose flour
- 2/3 cup clarified butter (vegetable oil optional)

PREPARATION

Sauté the onions in 1/2 of the butter (2 tablespoons) in a skillet over medium heat until they are translucent (1 minute). Then add the green peppers. When the green peppers begin to soften, add the red peppers and sauté until tender (about 2 minutes). Set the sautéed blend aside to cool.

Combine all the ingredients, except sautéed onion-pepper blend, the crabmeat and bread crumbs. Mix thoroughly and add the sautéed onion-pepper blend. Gently fold in the crabmeat to coat evenly. Then gently fold in the bread crumbs and salt and pepper to taste. Form the mixture into 2 ounce crabcakes (about 14 per recipe) and lightly coat with flour.

Sauté the crabcakes in clarified butter (or oil) over high heat until golden brown on both sides (about 1 1/2 minutes per side). Change clarified butter (or oil) between batches and wipe out pan, adding more clarified butter (or oil) between batches. Drain crabcakes on paper towels. Serve immediately. Serves about 4.

CHEF'S SUGGESTED MENU

Mesquite Grilled Fresh Porcini Mushrooms with Sautéed Baby Spinach, Crispy Leeks, Essence of Garlic and Fresh Rosemary

Salad of Exotic Baby Field Greens with Basil Leaves, Edible Rose Petals, Pommes Frites and a Sweet Basil Vinaigrette

Sautéed Maryland Crabcakes with a Roasted Red Pepper Beurre Blanc, Fresh Dill Aioli and Sweet Potato Hay

Pomegranate Grilled Colorado Lamb Chops with Roasted Garlic, Mashed Potatoes, Hummus Cakes, a Duet of Squash and Minted Lamb Jus

Individual Fresh Baked Apple Strudel with Creme Anglaise, Raspberry Coulis and Homemade Macadamia Nut Vanilla Ice Cream

We Welcome

Panico's

ITALIAN

Lunch Monday – Friday
Dinner Monday – Saturday
Closed Sundays
(Available for Parties)

Jackets Required for Gentlemen

Ample Self-Parking across the Street

Piano Music Weekends

Elegant Party Facilities

Wine Tasting Dinners

Off Premise Catering

*Accepts Diners Club and Other
Major Credit Cards*

**103 Church Street
New Brunswick, NJ
908.545.6100**

Established in 1987, Panico's is a sophisticated New Brunswick restaurant committed to excellence. It has been praised by the restaurant critics of *The New York Times* with the only "excellent" rating given to an Italian restaurant in 1993. It also received top billing in *The Star-Ledger* and is lauded by an army of repeat guests. Panico's is noted for the fine wines and classic and innovative Italian cuisine, plus a formally dressed legion of masterful unobtrusive servers. The artistically presented dishes, created by Executive Chef James Weaver using prime fresh ingredients, are splendid examples of Italian cuisine at its finest. Situated a short walk from Johnson & Johnson Corporate Headquarters, New Brunswick State Theater, George Street Playhouse and Crossroads Theater, Panico's luxurious ambiance and deluxe dining make it ideal for a romantic repast, pre-theater or business dinner.

Sole Pignolia

Ingredients

1/2 cup flour

2 pounds lemon sole filet

3 eggs, beaten

1 1/4 cups homemade bread crumbs mixed with 1 1/4 cups ground pignolia nuts

3 tablespoons butter

3/4 cup olive oil

Honey Lemon Sauce:
1 cup dry white wine

2 tablespoons honey

Juice of 1 lemon

1 shallot, diced

1/2 pound butter (cold)

Preparation

Preheat oven to 400° F. Lightly flour sole fillets, dip them in beaten egg and coat them in the bread crumb/pignolia nut mixture. In a large sauté pan, heat the butter and oil over medium heat until the butter is lightly browned. Add the fillets to the pan (if they do not fit, you'll have to do separate batches). Let them cook on each side until golden brown (approximately 2 minutes per side). Set fillets on a cookie sheet.

Honey lemon sauce: In a small sauce pan add wine, honey, lemon and shallot. Cook liquid until 1/4 cup remains. Remove from heat and whisk in butter a little at a time. Strain sauce over the fillets and serve immediately.

Chef's Suggested Menu

Carpaccio of Portobello Mushrooms

Pappardelle with Wild Mushrooms

Fillet of Sole Pignolia

Osso Buco of Turkey with Sun-Dried Cherries

Warm Mango Souffle with Slice Peaches and Honey Sauce

Ram's Head Inn

AMERICAN

Closed Mondays
Sunset Dinner Tuesday, Wednesday,
Thursday & Sunday
Outdoor Dining Facilities

Gentlemen: Jackets Please

Valet & Self-Parking

Piano Music in The Gallery
Art Showcase Lounge
Featuring Local Artists

Elegant Party Facilities
& Off Premise Catering

Accepts Diners Club and Other
Major Credit Cards

9 West White Horse Pike
Absecon, NJ
609.652.1700

Set on five country acres with sprawling gardens and flower-lined fences, Ram's Head Inn is unique in the area. Just eight miles from the bustling Atlantic City casinos, its wood-burning fireplaces and soft candlelight provide a respite for the senses and enhance the dining rooms, where traditional American specialties such as Pilgrim Creamy Chicken Pot Pie with Dumplings in a Copper Kettle and Glazed Crisp Roasted Duckling with Wild Rice are featured year round. Filled with authentic antiques and enhanced by a gracious courtyard, this delightful restaurant offers guests a chance to enjoy quiet, distinctively American dining in an elegant, country, cozy atmosphere. Among its many awards are AAA Four Diamonds and "Chefs in America." Ram's Head Inn has also been rated "Best of the Shore" by *Delaware Valley Magazine* and *Atlantic City Magazine*.

Pilgrim Creamy Chicken Pot Pie

Ingredients

For the chicken:
1 whole chicken (3 lbs.)
1 1/2 carrots (6 ounces)
1 celery rib
1/2 fresh onion (4 ounces)

For the dumplings:
1 cup flour
1/2 teaspoon baking powder
Salt to taste
2 tablespoons vegetable shortening
1/2 cup milk
2 cups chicken stock (from the boiled chicken)

For the Supreme sauce:
4 tablespoons butter
3/4 cup flour
2 cups chicken stock (from the boiled chicken)
2 cups barely simmering heavy cream
Salt and pepper to taste

For the assembly:
6 ounces fresh peas (or frozen)
6 ounces pearl onions, blanched (canned optional)
3/4 pound puff pastry
1 egg, beaten

Preparation

Make the chicken: Wash the chicken under cold running water. Place the chicken in a soup pot and cover with cold water. Add the carrots, celery and fresh onion. Bring to a boil over medium heat. Simmer over low heat for 25 minutes, skimming off the fat from the stock. Remove the chicken and carrots and let everything cool to room temperature. Skim the soup and use for other recipes. Remove skin and bones from the chicken and cut it into 3/4" pieces. Cut carrots into 1/2" pieces.

Make the dumplings: Combine the flour, baking powder and salt to taste. Add the shortening and beat with an electric mixer at low speed. Add milk and continue to mix gently until dough is smooth. Bring chicken stock to a boil over medium heat. Drop dough, one tablespoon at a time, into the boiling chicken stock. Cook over low heat for 10 minutes. Remove with slotted spoon, split in half and reserve.

Make the Supreme sauce: Melt the butter in a heavy-bottomed sauce pan over low heat. Sprinkle flour and mix well. Cook briefly, without allowing it color. Gradually add in chicken stock, whisking continuously. Simmer with occasional whisking over low heat for about 10 minutes. Remove from heat, add hot cream, whisk and return to low heat. Simmer over low heat with constant whisking until sauce is thickened. Pass sauce through a sieve into a warmed sauce pan. Add salt and pepper to taste.

Assemble: Place chicken, carrots, peas, blanched onions and two dumplings into individual casseroles and top with Supreme sauce. Roll out puff pastry. Cut dough in circles allowing a 1/2" overlap of the casserole rim. Brush bottom edge of pastry with beaten eggs and press pastry firmly over casserole. Brush top of pastry with eggs and bake in a preheated oven at 350°F for 20 to 25 minutes. Serve hot. Serves 4.

Chef's Suggested Menu

Maryland Crab Cake,
Dijon Mustard Sauce

Harvest Salad Walnuts,
Pears and Cheddar
on a Bed of Seasonal Greens,
Balsamic Vinaigrette

Pilgrim Creamy Chicken Pot Pie
in a Copper Kettle

Apple-Cranberry Cobbler

RAM'S HEAD INN

We Welcome
Diners Club International

Rod's 1890's Restaurant

AMERICAN/CONTINENTAL

Lunch Monday – Saturday
Dinner Every Day
Fabulous Sunday Brunch
Closed Christmas Day
Early Evening Menu

Country Club Casual

Valet & Self-Parking

Nightly Entertainment & Dancing

Party Facilities

Accepts Diners Club and Other Major Credit Cards

Route 24
Convent Station, NJ
201.539.6666

Rod's 1890's Restaurant was conceived and developed by the Keller family more than 56 years ago — and it has been pleasing patrons under the Keller management ever since. Situated near the site of the elegant estates of the 1890's, this charming dining establishment is one of the most refined theme restaurants on the East coast. Victorian ambiance created by an abundance of priceless antiques lends a touch of class to a value-oriented dining experience at Rod's. The masterful kitchen staff skillfully prepares consistently good dishes using top quality ingredients like its aged prime beef, freshly caught lobsters and superior fresh fish. The diverse wine selection is splendid, the desserts are seductive and the proficient service staff assures satisfaction.

Rack of Lamb, Prisille

Ingredients

A whole rack of lamb (8 chops)

Fresh ground black pepper

Salt

1/2 teaspoon thyme

1 tablespoon minced fresh garlic (or garlic powder)

1/4 cup dijon mustard

8 tablespoons sweet butter, melted

2 cups of fresh bread crumbs

Preparation

Have the butcher prepare the lamb for roasting (frenching). Cover the ends of each bone to prevent charring. Sprinkle the lamb with pepper, salt and thyme to taste Place meat in a roasting pan in a preheated oven at 400° F and cook for 15 minutes.

Remove the lamb and allow to stand until cool enough to handle. Rub the meat surfaces with minced garlic. Spread the meat surfaces with mustard and brush with melted butter.

Spread the bread crumbs (prepared by mincing fresh white bread in a food processor) on a foil sheet. Press the meat into the crumbs and return the roast to the oven for about another 15 to 17 minutes (medium rare). Allow the roast to stand for about 5 minutes before carving.

Serve with mint jelly, blanched, buttered string beans and boiled, small new potatoes or couscous. Serves 4.

Chef's Suggested Menu

Maryland Crab Cakes

Caesar Salad

Rack of Spring Lamb Prisille

Chocolate Marquis, Creme Fraiche

Rod's 1890's Restaurant

We Welcome Diners Club International

Rudolfo Ristorante

ITALIAN

*Lunch Monday – Friday
Dinner Every Day*

Jackets Required

Self-Parking

*Elegant Facilities for Private Parties
& Corporate Functions*

*Accepts Diners Club and Other
Major Credit Cards*

---

12 LACKAWANNA AVENUE
PEAPACK-GLADSTONE, NJ
908.781.1888

PRACTICALLY HIDDEN ON A SIDE STREET IN THE TINY RURAL TOWN OF GLADSTONE, THE HANDSOME ITALIAN RISTORANTE NAMED RUDOLFO ATTRACTS LEGIONS OF REGULARS BECAUSE IT PROVIDES AN EXCEPTIONAL DINING EXPERIENCE. TRUE TO THE HERITAGE OF THE "MOTHER CUISINE OF EUROPE," RUDOLFO'S AUTHENTIC ITALIAN FARE IS SUBTLE, SEEMINGLY EFFORTLESS AND VERY ELEGANT. THE MANAGEMENT IS SERIOUS ABOUT WINES, PROVIDING AN EXTENSIVE SET OF BOTTLES THAT ARE IDEAL COMPANIONS FOR THE COOKERY. EXCELLENT CUISINE, FINE WINES AND AN UNPRETENTIOUS SERVICE STAFF THAT IS SKILLFUL AND ADEPT AT PLEASING PATRONS ARE MATCHED WITH STATELY, HANDSOME SURROUNDINGS AKIN TO THE DINING ROOM OF AN ITALIAN COUNTRY VILLA. SPECIALTIES LIKE OSSOBUCCO MILANESE ARE A PERFECT EXAMPLE OF COUNTRY ITALIAN COOKING AT ITS FINEST, AND THE SINFUL DESSERTS ARE A GREAT EXCUSE TO ABUSE THE WAISTLINE AT THIS STELLAR COUNTRY ITALIAN RISTORANTE.

Red Snapper Alla Rudolfo

Ingredients

2 filets of fresh red snapper (about 3/4 pounds each)

1/8 cup olive oil

Dry white wine to just cover (3/4 to 1 cup)

1/2 peeled seeded fresh tomato, chopped (1/2 cup)

6 pitted black olives, diced (1/4 cup)

1/8 cup capers

3 cups loosely packed fresh arugula, blanched for 15 seconds in boiling water, refreshed in cold water and squeezed dry

3 tablespoons extra virgin olive oil

1 clove garlic, minced

1/4 cup lightly toasted pignolia nuts (optional)

Preparation

Brush fish with olive oil and place fish in baking dish. Add dry white wine to barely cover. Top the fish with tomatoes, olives and capers. Bake the fish in a preheated oven at 475° F until it is white and just cooked through (about 7 to 10 minutes).

Place arugula, extra virgin olive oil, garlic and pignolia nuts in the bowl of a food processor. Pureé until very smooth. Place pureéd arugula on two warmed plates.

Remove the red snapper and place on the pureéd arugula. Serve with a wedge of lemon. Serves 2.

Chef's Suggested Menu

~

Seared Portobello Mushrooms Seasoned with Truffle Oil

Housemade Butternut Squash Ravioli with Zucchini and Walnuts, Garlic and Extra Virgin Olive Oil

Red Snapper Alla Rudolfo

Fresh Lemon Tart

~

Rudolfo

The Ryland Inn

FRENCH

Lunch Monday – Friday
Dinner Every Day

Gentlemen: Jackets Please

*Elegant Private, Wedding &
Corporate Party & Meeting
Facilities: Indoors & Outdoors*

Picnic Facilities

*Helipad Landing Facilities
(Call in Advance)*

Accepts Diners Club and Other
Major Credit Cards

ROUTE 22 WEST
WHITEHOUSE, NJ
908.534.4011

The Ryland Inn, a captivating restaurant situated on 50 manicured acres in Hunterdon County, is a perfect setting for the world-class cuisine of Craig Shelton and his masterful staff of distinguished chefs. Mr. Shelton, who has worked with internationally renowned chefs such as Alain Chapel, Joel Robuchon and Paul Haeberland in France and Wolfgang Puck in California, skillfully integrates the contemporary and regional cuisines of France and America in an alluring array of enchanting, refined dishes which are complemented by an award-winning selection of wines. This deluxe dining spot attracts an urbane corporate clientele and a legion of sophisticated serious diners eager to taste food seldom encountered in these parts. Mr. Shelton's unique chef's tasting menus, designed to match individual tastes and preferences in food and wine, are beguiling feasts guaranteed to create enduring memories.

Roast Chicken with Roasted Vegetables

Ingredients

For the roast chicken:
8 whole unpeeled shallots

12 unpeeled pearl onions

2 whole cloves unpeeled garlic

1 whole fresh chicken (3 lbs.), cleaned, wiped dry (inside and out) with paper towels

Roasting herbs (1 sprig rosemary, 2 sprigs thyme and 1 bay leaf)

Grey sea salt (or regular salt)

Fresh milled white pepper

2 tablespoons vegetable oil

4 tablespoons sweet butter

Lardons (12 small cubes, 1" long, 1/4" wide of bacon)

6 small new potatoes (1/2 lb.)

Rock salt to cover potatoes (kosher salt optional)

2 large carrots, cleaned and cut into rounds the size of the shallots (1 cup)

2 tablespoon sweet butter

For the sauce:
2 tablespoons sherry vinegar

2/3 cup chicken consommea

Pinch fresh rosemary, thyme

Few drops of truffle oil

Preparation

Make the roast chicken: Roast shallots, pearl onions and garlic in a preheated oven at 225° F until tender without developing color on any side. Remove, cool, peel and reserve. Stuff chicken with one roasted garlic clove and roasting herbs. Season inside and outside with grey sea salt and white pepper. Tuck tail inside cavity and truss tightly.

Sear all sides in vegetable oil and roast in preheated oven at 350° F with basting butter and lardons. Baste often. Make sure no water accumulates in the roasting pan. If so, turn up heat a bit for 1 1/2 to 2 hours. Roast potatoes, covered in rock salt and covered in foil, in preheated oven at 350° F until soft (about 50 minutes). Remove, slice and keep in warm place covered by a damp towel.

During the last 5 minutes of roasting chicken, add carrots, roasted onions, shallots and remaining clove of garlic. Remove chicken, rest neck down, reserve vegetables in pan.

Make the sauce: Deglaze roasting pan with vinegar, combine with rest of ingredients (**vegetables and potatoes**) and boil to reduce in half (5 minutes on top of stove).

Assemble: Cut chicken in half, reheat and serve with vegetables, roasting herbs and potatoes tossed in remaining butter heated to foaming. Arrange meat and vegetables over sauce. Serves 2.

Chef's Suggested Menu

∾

Terrine of Foie Gras with Sautérnes

Steamed Black Sea Bass with Three Celeries

Roasted Chicken and Vegetables with Tarragon

Rotisserie Pigeon and Grilled Foie Gras, Asparagus Morels and Cabbage

Strawberry Soup with Sweet Vouvray and Sorbets

∾

The Ryland Inn

Sammy's
Ye Old Cider Mill

AMERICAN/STEAKHOUSE

*Open for Dinner Only
Wednesday – Monday
Closed Tuesdays*

Casual Dress

Self-Parking

Party Facilities

*Accepts Diners Club and Other
Major Credit Cards*

ROUTE 24 WEST
MENDHAM, NJ
201.543.7675

*S*AMMY'S YE OLD CIDER MILL DOESN'T ADVERTISE AND THERE ISN'T A SAMMY'S SIGN OUT FRONT TO SIGNIFY "THIS IS THE PLACE." THE LOYAL, SOPHISTICATED CLIENTELE WHO THRONG TO THIS UNIQUE QUINTESSENTIAL ROADSIDE RESTAURANT DON'T NEED SIGNS OR FANCY DECOR. THEY SIMPLY YEARN FOR SAMMY'S MAGNIFICENT DRY-AGED BLACK ANGUS MELTINGLY-TENDER PRIME T-BONE STEAKS THAT STREAM RIVULETS OF SCRUMPTIOUS JUICES AT THE CUT OF A KNIFE, LOBSTERS THAT TASTE LIKE THEY WERE PLUCKED FROM THE MAINE WATERS, ENORMOUS CUTS OF LAMB CHOPS, FABULOUS SHOESTRING FRIES AND FARM FRESH VEGETABLES THAT VARY WITH THE SEASON. THE *ZAGAT TRI-STATE RESTAURANT SURVEY* LISTED THE ATTRACTIONS AT SAMMY'S AS: "BIG PORTIONS OF GREAT STEAK AND FRIES, AND THE BEST LOBSTER." SAMMY'S OUTLIVED MOST OTHER RESTAURANTS AND THE PROHIBITION ERA TO BECOME A LEGEND IN THESE PARTS, BECAUSE IT SERVES ITS CLIENTELE THE BEST AND DOESN'T WORRY ABOUT THE REST.

Mustard Sauce

Ingredients

1 1/2 cups thick, homemade mayonnaise (Hellmann's optional)

1/2 cup Polish mustard (Kosciusko optional)

1 1/2 tablespoon of light yellow prepared mustard (French's)

1/4 cup prepared horseradish (Axelrod's)

Juice of 1/2 a large lemon

4 dashes Worcestershire sauce (Lee & Perrins)

Preparation

Whisk together the ingredients, one at a time, in the order listed. Place in a glass bowl, cover with plastic wrap, and refrigerate.

The stone crab, prized for its luscious sweet claw meat is an authentic American gourmet food, air-shipped from Miami to stellar restaurants all over the world. During the season, from October to March, you will find some of the largest, most succulent specimens at Sammy's. At this legendary restaurant – where the finest, prime quality ingredients are treasured as the cornerstone of its cuisine – the luscious taste of firm, snowy claw meat of the stone crab is amplified by a distinctive mustard sauce developed by Sammy himself. This savory mayonnaise-based sauce (which may be prepared with the suggested brand-name commercial ingredients) will also flatter the intrinsic taste of poached fresh salmon.

Chef's Suggested Menu

~

Steamed Stone Crab Claws, Mustard Sauce

Tossed Seasonal Salad, Vinaigrette

Charred Prime T-Bone Steak with Steamed Maine Lobster, Shoestring Fries and Seasonal Garden-Fresh Vegetables

Deep Dish Apple Pie

~

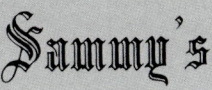

Sestri Caffe & Ristorante

ITALIAN

Lunch Monday – Friday
Dinner Every Day

Proper Attire in Caffe
Jackets in Formal Dining Room

Self-Parking

Weekend Piano Music in Caffe

Elegant Party Facilities
& Corporate Functions

Accepts Diners Club and Other
Major Credit Cards

342 Valley Road
Gillette, NJ
908.647.0697

Aldo Marsiglia left a senior management position at one of New York's highly rated restaurants to create Sestri, which takes its name from Aldo's hometown on the Italian Riviera. At Sestri, this seasoned restaurateur dedicates himself to consistently providing a top quality Italian dining experience in an attractive country restaurant with two distinct dining moods. Weekdays, the beamed-ceiling cafe is a rustic setting for casual, yet elegant dining; weekend guests often choose the ambiance in the formal dining room, which replicates a sophisticated Ligurian country villa. In either setting, diners encounter the same highly professional, proficient service as they experience food and wine that take them on a culinary journey tasting the unique cuisines of the various regions of Italy. Little wonder that Sestri rates as one of the best Italian restaurants in Northern New Jersey in the *Zagat Tri-State Restaurant Survey.*

Pollo Sestrino

Ingredients

4 whole skinless and boneless chicken breasts, halved

Flour to coat chicken

1/2 cup vegetable oil

1 tablespoon unsalted butter

1/2 cup dry white wine

1/4 cup sun-dried tomatoes, packed in olive oil, drained and coarsely chopped

1/4 cup Gaeta black olives, pitted and halved

1/2 cup chicken broth

Salt and fresh ground black pepper to taste

5 to 6 fresh basil leaves (optional)

Preparation

Lightly coat chicken with flour. Heat oil in large, heavy skillet over medium-high heat until hot. Sauté chicken in batches on both sides until lightly browned (about 3 minutes each side). Transfer chicken breasts to warm plate. Discard cooking oil.

Add butter, wine, sun-dried tomatoes and olives to skillet and cook with constant stirring for 1 minute. Add chicken broth and simmer over low heat until the sauce thickens slightly (about 2 minutes). Add salt and pepper to taste. Return chicken to skillet and heat for 2 minutes.

Place chicken on a warm serving platter and spoon sauce over the breasts. Garnish with basil leaves and serve immediately. Serves 4.

Chef's Suggested Menu

Prosciutto Con Mozzarella e Melanzane
(Parma prosciutto with fresh mozzarella and marinated eggplant)

Trenette al pesto
(homemade thin noodles tossed with Genoa's world renown pesto sauce)

Gamberoni "Ca Di Ferrei"
(jumbo shrimp bathed in a light mustard sauce)

Pollo Sestrino
(breast of chicken with sun-dried tomatoes and Gaeta olives)

Frutti Di Bosco Con Zabaglione Freddo Allo Champagne
(seasonal berries with cold zabaglione)

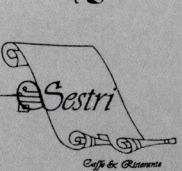

SING YA

CHINESE

*Lunch daily
Dinner Every Day*

Country Club Casual

Self-Parking

*Elegant Private Party Facilities
for Meeting, Gourmet
Dinners & Weddings*

*Accepts Diners Club and Other
Major Credit Cards*

---

520 SYLVAN AVENUE
ENGLEWOOD CLIFFS, NJ
201.568.9855

THE explosive growth of CHINESE restaurants spawned precious few distinctive urbane dining spots equal to the likes of SING YA. Its renditions of the multi-faceted authentic cuisines of CANTON, PEKING and the other gastronomic regions of CHINA are wondrous. These creations, seldom seen in these environs, are presented with matching wines and unique beers in beautiful surroundings by highly professional servers led by fluent captains that help patrons compose a provocative gourmet dinner suited to their tastes. SING YA'S epicurean delights includes unique starters like steamed fresh scallops, oysters and abalone in shells bathed with savory black bean sauce. Its distinctive main dishes include sumptuous fare like braised shark's fin with crab meat, prawns and sea scallops in a taro nest and spicy deep-fried sesame chicken. SING YA will take you on a culinary journey to the birthplace of the world's oldest gourmet cuisine.

Lobster Cantonese Style

Ingredients

Mixture A:

3 tablespoons minced scallions

2 1/2 tablespoons fermented black beans, rinsed, drained and minced

2 tablespoons minced garlic

1 tablespoon peeled minced fresh ginger

Mixture B:

1/2 pound ground pork

2 teaspoons soy sauce

1 teaspoon Chinese rice wine (or sake)

1/2 teaspoon sesame oil

Mixture C:

1 1/2 cups chicken broth

2 1/2 tablespoons soy sauce

2 tablespoons rice wine (or sake)

1 teaspoon sesame sauce

1/2 teaspoon sugar

1/2 teaspoon white pepper

Mixture D:

2 tablespoons cornstarch, mix well with 1/4 cup water

Mixture E:

3 large eggs, beaten lightly

Other Ingredients:

2 two pound live lobsters

2 tablespoons peanut oil

Preparation

Prepare Mixtures A, B, C, D and E (mixing ingredients listed and beating eggs) in separate bowls. Prepare the lobster by splitting each along underside (head to tail) and discarding intestines, sacs near head, eyes, short legs along tail and antennae. Cut the lobster, through shell, into 1/2 " pieces.

Heat oil in wok over high heat (until almost smoking). Add Mixture A and stir-fry for 15 seconds. Add Mixture B and stir-fry for 1 minute until pork loses pink color. Add lobster pieces and stir-fry 1 minute and add Mixture C. Bring to a boil, cover and simmer for 3 minutes. Remove cover and stir in Mixture D.

Simmer the blend with frequent stirring until liquid is slightly thickened. Add Mixture E (the eggs) in a steady stream, stirring, and remove from heat. Toss until everything is well combined. Transfer to a large heated serving dish, sprinkle top with minced scallions and serve with steamed rice. Serves 6.

Chef's Suggested Menu

**Mixed Appetizers:
Steamed Oysters on Half Shell
with Black Bean Sauce,
Deep-Fried Seafood Rolls,
Stuffed Conch with Minced Seafood,
Pan-fried Dumplings**

Diced Fillet of Fish Soup

Lobster Cantonese Style

Roast Squab

**Braised Sea Bass
with Shredded Pork,
Sautéed Mustard Greens**

**A Melange of
Fresh Seasonal Fruit**

VALENTINO'S

ITALIAN

Valentino's:
Lunch Monday – Friday
Dinner Daily

150 South:
Open Monday – Saturday
11 AM – 1:30 AM

Country Club Casual

Self-Parking in Rear Lot

Private Party & Meeting Facilities

Accepts Diners Club and Other
Major Credit Cards

**150 SOUTH STREET
MORRISTOWN, NJ
201.993.8066**

Valentino's enviable reputation and loyal following has flourished because it has oodles of attributes. Its classic and modern Italian cuisine is on the mark, its selection of top value wines is top-drawer, the servers are polished and the ambiance is warm and cordial. Valentino's embraces the engaging custom of wheeling a service trolley heaped with a cornucopia of cold antipasti through the dining room and serving herbal extra virgin olive oil with its crusty Tuscan bread. The simply scrumptious pastas are homemade, the main dishes utterly satisfying and desserts are beguiling. Recently, Valentino's introduced 150 South, situated adjacent to the restaurant (accessible from outside and Valentino's dining room). This stylish addition features sophisticated music on an elegant baby grand piano and a beautiful mahogany bar for cocktails and light Italian fare to complement its romantic setting. Both 150 South and Valentino's are as captivating as its famous silent film namesake.

Penne Bisanzio

Ingredients

- 20 medium size fresh plum tomatoes
- 4 large cloves garlic, peeled and sliced thin
- 2 tablespoons dried oregano
- 1/2 cup extra virgin olive oil
- Salt and fresh ground pepper to taste
- 6 quarts rapidly boiling water with a tablespoon of salt
- 1 pound penne (quill-shaped pasta)
- 3/4 cup coarsely chopped fresh mozzarella cheese
- 2 bunches fresh basil, cut into coarse pieces (about 6 cups)

Preparation

Add tomatoes to a large pot of boiling water (about 5 quarts) and cook for 30 seconds. Remove tomatoes and place in pot of ice water. Cool for 2 minutes, remove and drain. Peel tomatoes, cut cross-wise and remove seeds. Chop tomatoes into 1/2" cubes, place in glass bowl with garlic, oregano and olive oil. Add salt and fresh ground pepper to taste. Mix well and cover with plastic film. Refrigerate overnight (optional minimum time 1 hour). Place contents of bowl in large sauté pan and cook over medium heat for 10 minutes.

A few minutes before starting to cook the sauce, gradually add penne to boiling salted water. Boil uncovered for about 10 minutes until tender, but still firm. Drain. Toss penne with sauce in sauté pan over medium heat, add chopped mozzarella cheese and basil and mix well. Serve immediately, garnished with fresh basil leaves (optional). Serves 4 to 6.

Chef's Suggested Menu

Bruschetta Polenta Gorgonzola
(squares of polenta topped with melted gorgonzola cheese)

Penne Bisanzio

Costolette alla Milanese Topped with Arugula, Tomatoes and Red Onions in a Balsamic Vinaigrette
(large veal cutlets coated lightly with crumbs, fried and topped with arugula, tomatoes and red onions in a balsamic vinaigrette)

Classic Italian Cheesecake

Valentino's

Villa Amalfi

ITALIAN

Lunch Tuesday – Friday
Dinner Tuesday – Sunday
Sunset Dinner Tuesday – Friday

Jackets for Gentlemen

Live Entertainment in the Lounge
Wednesdays, Fridays & Saturdays

Valet Parking

Elegant Corporate
& Private Party Facilities

Accepts Diners Club and Other
Major Credit Cards

793 Palisades Avenue
Cliffside Park, NJ
201.886.8626

Villa Amalfi, rated highly for its food, decor and service in the *Zagat Tri-State Restaurant Survey*, is an urbane ristorante with a provocative blend of classic and contemporary Italian cuisine coupled with tantalizing Continental delights like Beluga caviar and steak tartare. Service by a bevy of formally dressed professionals is masterful and the wine cellar is stocked with a judicious assortment of bottles that match the elegant cucina. The diverse, homemade pasta options include elegant dishes such as ravioli filled with lobster and served with a silky cream sauce and risotto with porcini mushrooms. The attractive main dish presentations include lots of old standbys as well as inventive creations like red snapper baked in a light vinaigrette accented with herbs and sautéed filet of sole under a blanket of diced tomatoes enhanced with almonds and herbs.

Fusilli with Vodka and Caviar

Ingredients

- 1 pound fusilli
- 1 tablespoon extra virgin olive oil
- 4 tablespoons sweet butter
- 1 tablespoon shallots, chopped
- 4 plum tomatoes, peeled, seeded and diced
- 1/4 cup vodka
- 2 cups heavy cream
- Salt and pepper to taste
- 1/2 cup grated Romano cheese
- 3 tablespoons salmon caviar

Preparation

Add fusilli to large pot with 5 quarts of boiling salted water. Cook until firm to the bite (about 12 minutes). Drain, place in large bowl and toss with olive oil. Reserve.

In a large skillet over medium heat, melt the butter. Add the shallots and sauté until soft, but not brown. Add the plum tomatoes and simmer for 3 minutes. Add the vodka and simmer for 3 minutes more. Add the heavy cream and simmer for 5 minutes more. Add salt and pepper to taste. Pour the cooked fusilli into skillet and mix well. Add the grated cheese and toss to coat evenly. Cook for another 2 minutes and place the pasta in a large heated platter. Garnish with caviar.

Chef's Suggested Menu

Calamari Luciana
(small squid stuffed and served with a light brown sauce)

Insalate Tricolore
(radicchio, arugula and endive tossed with a balsamic vinaigrette)

Fusilli with Vodka and Caviar

Salmone al Chablis
(Norwegian salmon fillet, artichoke hearts and capers in a chablis sauce)

**Black Forest Torte;
Raspberry Sauce**

WASHINGTON INN

AMERICAN/CONTEMPORARY

*Open for Dinner Every Day
Patio & Porch Dining*

Dress Code

Self-Parking

Nightly Piano Music

Elegant Party Facilities

*Accepts Diners Club and Other
Major Credit Cards*

---

801 WASHINGTON STREET
CAPE MAY, NJ
609.884.5697

Numerous honors have been heaped on the Washington Inn, situated in a handsomely restored 1840's plantation in the heart of Cape May. It received a three-star rating by the critics of *New Jersey Monthly*, who labeled this place "a most enchanting spot". The Washington Inn was also chosen by the readers of *New Jersey Monthly* as the "Best of the Best" in the "Readers' Choice Awards" in 1992 and 1993. Recognizing the extraordinary depth and breadth of its wine cellar, *The Wine Spectator* gave the Washington Inn its "Award of Excellence". The Washington Inn's imaginative Contemporary American cuisine, a menu that changes with the seasons, includes delectable dishes and simply scrumptious desserts that are beautifully presented and skillfully served in romantic dining rooms with cozy fireplaces to warm hearts during the winter months.

CAPE MAY MONKFISH
WITH HORSERADISH CRUST
AND MUSTARD SAUCE

INGREDIENTS

For the mustard sauce:
1 finely chopped shallot
1 cup white wine
2 teaspoons champagne vinegar
4 tablespoons whole grain dijon mustard
1 pound cold sweet butter cut into small pieces
Salt and pepper to taste

For the monkfish:
2 1/2 pounds fresh monkfish
Flour for dusting
1 cup sweet butter, softened
1 cup dijon mustard
6 tablespoons grated horseradish (jar-type option)
Salt and pepper to taste
2 cups fresh bread crumbs
3 tablespoons olive oil

PREPARATION

Note: Monkfish is always plentiful in southern New Jersey as scallop fishermen catch them in their dredges. It has a delicate, sweet taste because it feeds on shellfish, thus it's known as the "poor man's lobster".

Place shallots, white wine, vinegar and mustard in small non-reactive saucepan. Bring to a boil over medium heat and simmer until the liquid is almost evaporated (about 2 tablespoons left). Reduce the heat to moderately low and whisk in the butter, one piece at a time, lifting the skillet from the heat occasionally to cool the mixture and adding each new pieces of butter before the previous one has melted completely. The sauce should not get hot enough to liquefy. It should be thin enough to coat the back of a spoon. Season with salt and pepper and keep warm.

Make the monkfish: Cut monkfish into 10 2" thick medallions and lightly coat with all-purpose flour. Combine butter, mustard, horseradish, a pinch of salt and pepper and bread crumbs in a bowl. Blend well.

Heat olive oil in large skillet over medium high heat. Sear monkfish on both sides and remove to a baking sheet. Top with crumb mixture and bake in a preheated 350° F oven for about 12 minutes until golden.

Assemble: Place mustard sauce on serving place, arrange monkfish over sauce and garnish with chopped parsley and slices of fresh lemon. Serves 5.

CHEF'S SUGGESTED MENU

Oyster and Roasted Red Pepper Bisque

Watercress and Endive Salad with Goat Cheese and Fresh Herb Dressing

Champagne Sorbet

Cape May Monkfish with Horseradish Crust and Mustard Sauce

Almond Basket Filled with Wild Berries and French Creme

INGLENOOK
LASTING IMPRESSIONS
SINCE 1879

Choosing the Right Wine:
Errors, Terrors, and Pleasures*

by Tom Maresca

Matching food and wine can't be much of a mystery; if it were, the human race wouldn't have made it this far. The fact is, however, that for many people today choosing a wine to partner with a particular meal is a mystery – for the simple reason that, for the very first time, a blessedly large segment of the human race actually has a choice about what it eats and drinks.

In the past, there was no food-and-wine matching problem because there were no options. You ate what your own or nearby farms grew, fatted and slaughtered your own pigs, grew and fermented your own grapes, and drank the wine of the country, whatever color it was, with whatever you ate. Now, we can choose from the harvests of fields and forests and vineyards from all over the globe: Our food could be Caribbean or Cajun, Chinese or Classic French, Italian or Indian – East, West, or Native American – and our vin de pays can hail from New York or California, Connecticut or Texas, Europe or Australia, South Africa or South America. None of the components of our dinner may ever have met each other before. They might not have dwelt on the same continent before we joined them in wedlock on a plate. No wonder choosing a wine to go with them is troublesome: They don't even speak the same language.

That's the worst of it, however. The good news is that matching wines and foods doesn't involve a whole lot of mysterious lore. You don't need the equivalent of a college major or post-graduate courses to be able to choose a decent dinner wine for yourself and your family and friends. All you have to do is pay attention to a few things that you may not have given much thought to up till now.

Understanding what makes wine and food compatible amounts to little more than noticing, verbalizing, and reducing to a remembarable system what happens on your palate when you taste a particular food along with a particular wine. Consistent pleasure in wine and food matching depends on nothing more difficult than finding out why certain foods and wine combinations please or displease you, and then learning how to generalize from that simple information.

A Loaf of Bread, A Jug of Wine, and Thou

As with almost every other kind of knowledge, the key first steps are simply learning what to pay attention to: what factors in the food, what elements in the wine, what facets of your taste are going to make a difference. What is at stake in any wine and food pairing is always the same trinity of variables: the nature of the wine, the nature of the food, and the preferences of the taster.

Difficulties arise only when the three elements fall out of balance, when one is more sophisticated, or much less sophisticated, than the others. This is particularly true with regard to the preferences of the tasters and their awareness of them, since the whole process of wine matching – and wine enjoyment – is so utterly subjective. Gustatory heaven – the "perfect meal," that

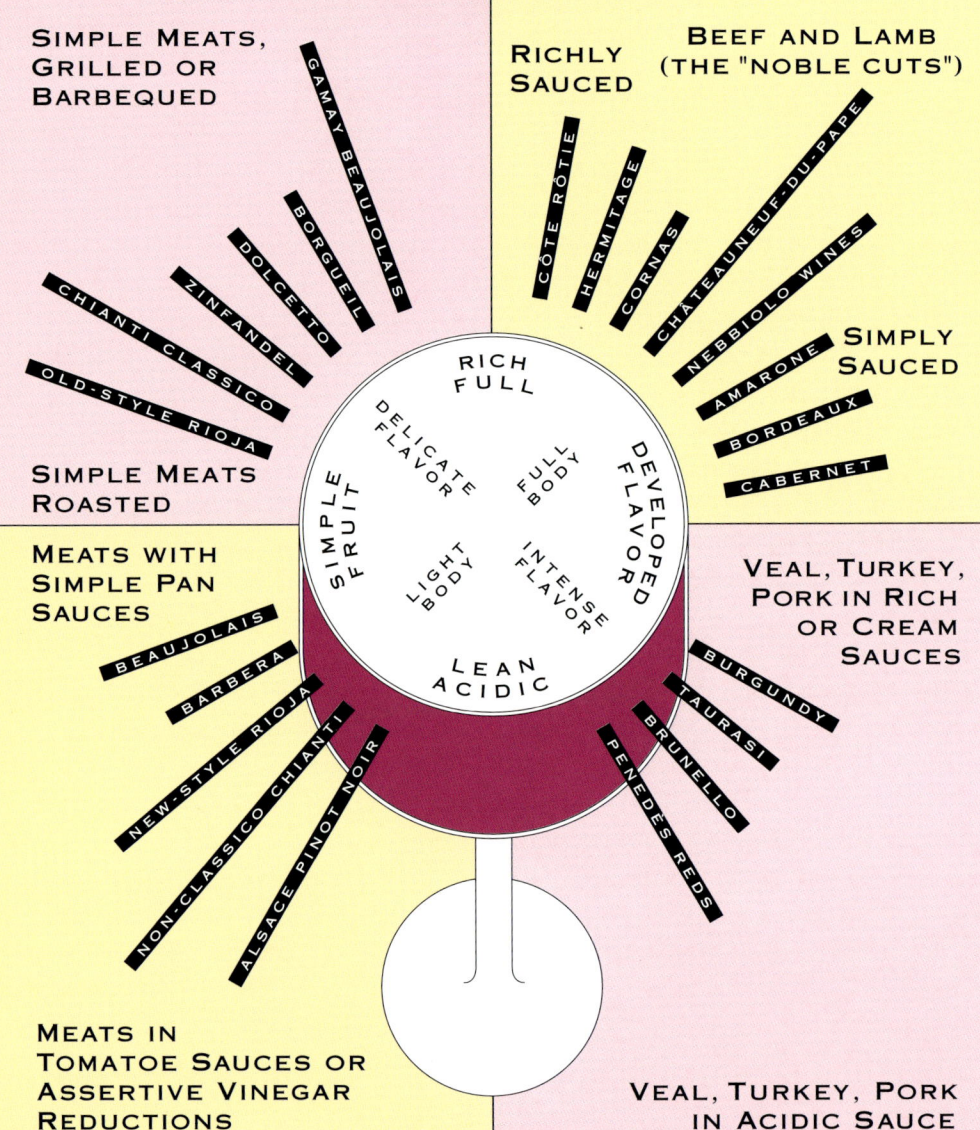

which you can't imagine anything better – comes about when all three elements mesh exactly, when the wine presents rich and complex flavors that complement the harmony of the foods, and when your palate can appreciate everything the wine and food have to offer. Just as a wine that falls below the occasion and the cuisine is bound to disappoint you, so too a wine above and beyond your palatal range will never be fully enjoyable for you, no matter how many gold medals it's won or how much you pay for it or how impressively it's served. You eat only with your own mouth; you taste only with your own palate. The wisdom of knowing yourself, realizing as objectively as you can your own abilities and limitations, preferences and aversions, applies just as much to wining and dining as it does to any other physical and mental activity.

Ten Commandments for Wine-Lovers

Here are some very basic guidelines to aid you in choosing wines to match your your meals. Remember, they operate as guidelines only, not as inviolable laws. They are useful because they derive from the nature of various foods and wines themselves.

1. There is no such animal as the single right wine for a particular food or dish.
2. Personal preference overrides any other rules we may generate, unless that preference makes life and dinner miserable for others at the table.
3. The wines for everyday meals should be relatively simple, dry, and inexpensive.

The first two vinous commandments stipulate that there is no such thing as a strange god. You can worship what wine you please: The wine you like is the right wine for you. As long as you're choosing only for yourself and others of compatible tastes, personal preference amounts to the dominant consideration in any everyday wine-and-food pairing, even to the point of overriding the third guideline.

Tastes are rarely identical, however, even within the same family, and the point at which they are most likely to divide is sugar: the amount of sweetness each individual finds pleasant or even tolerable. Many people – I, for instance, am one – have no sweet tooth at all. I don't like very sweet desserts, and although I can relish – in small quantities – some very sweet dessert wines, I can't tolerate any sweetness at all in the wines I drink with my dinner. Many other wine-drinkers – most of them, perhaps – have this same low tolerance for sweetness. That is because the sugar in a sweet wine acts as a muffler of other flavors. It creates a baffle that prevents the real tastes of food from reaching you palate. Now, I like the tastes of food. I want to be able to perceive and enjoy the different flavors of the various ingredients in the dishes I choose, whether those flavors are subtle or striking, so I want a wine that will enhance those flavors rather than blur them together. Ergo, rule of thumb 3: everyday wine should be simple because most everyday foods are simple, dry so you can actually taste the good flavors that are in them and the foods you drink them with, and inexpensive so that you can enjoy them without pain.

4. The nature of the food and the nature of the wine, along with the preferences of the tasters, should determine the choice of a wine.

White Wine Food Wheel

Richly Sauced Seafood
- Dry Chenin Blanc
- Simple Chablis
- Pouilly-Fumé
- Sauvignon Blanc

Lobster, Crab

Richly Sauced White Meats
- Chardonnay
- White Burgundy
- White Rhône

Pork, Turkey

Richly Sauced Fowl

Veal
- Muscadet
- Verdicchio
- New-Style White Rioja
- New-Style White Graves
- Pinot Grigio
- Soave
- German Kabinett Wines

Simply Prepared Fowl
- Alsace Whites
- Old-Style White Rioja
- Greco di Tufo
- Tocai
- Old-Style Graves

Raw Shellfish

Simply Prepared Finfish

Center wheel:
- RICH / FULL
- DELICATE FLAVOR
- FULL BODY
- DEVELOPED FLAVOR
- SIMPLE FRUIT
- LIGHT BODY
- INTENSE FLAVOR
- LEAN / ACIDIC

Adapted from The Right Wine *by Tom Maresca © 1990.*

Rule 4 simply spells out the three factors that you have to take account of in any wine and food match-up: you may very well already do this automatically, without even thinking about it, but this trio needs to have some conscious attention devoted to it. The remaining guidelines are designed to draw out exactly what these three items involve.

5. Self-knowledge is crucial: tasters must be aware of their own palatal preferences, skills, or limitations.

Number five requires you to pay attention to the nature of your own biases and blind spots, which will not necessarily coincide with anybody else's. Start with the obvious things: is anyone a vegetarian? allergic to anything? does anyone eat only Kosher, or nothing but fish? Is anybody sensitive to sulfites? Then you might have a problem with white wines. To histamines? Then you might have a problem with reds. Are there any positive predilections you want to honor? For example: Do your guests or family all dote on big, red wines? If so, then you might want such a wine even with a dish you would ordinarily consider too delicate to serve with a robust wine. Are they real white wine fans? Then you might want to try serving them not only wines they already know but some they might not have tried yet – Alsace Pinot Gris rather than Chardonnay, Marsanne or Tocai rather than Sauvignon. These are gross instances: Many more subtle ones are possible – people who love or hate specific kinds of wine, like Riesling or Sauvignon or Cabernet for instance.

6. Match foods and wines according to the components that dominate in their actual taste and texture, not in their menu description or ingredient list or nutritional or chemical analysis.
7. In most dinners, the main dish should indicate the wine to be served with the entire meal.
8. "Red wine with red meat, white wine with white meat, fowl, or fish" makes a lot of sense, but it should never be taken as an absolute rule.
9. Strongly flavored dishes will normally need an equally strongly flavored wine to accompany them: usually this will indicate a red wine.
10. Mildly flavored dishes require a more delicate wine to accompany them: normally this will indicate a white wine.

Guideline six gives you the key points you should look to in the foods and wines you are considering pairing, and numbers seven through ten focus with increasing sharpness on the single most important objective determinant in the whole situation, the character of the central dish or course. This, more than any other single factor (save only strong personal preference) should determine your choice of wine. And where sets of taste buds other than your own are involved, this, more than any other factor, will determine the success or failure of your wine-and-food matching. The nature of the central dish or main course contains most of the clues you need to choose a compatible wine, a wine that "goes with" the food.

From this common-sensical observation flow all the esoteric principles you'll ever need to successfully pair wines and foods. Whether you want a wine that will simply accompany your dinner without fuss or fanfare, or you want a wine to dress that dinner up and make it special, or

you want a dinner that will show off a particular wine to best advantage, the main dish or main course provides all the clues you will need – even for those three very different goals. This guideline presupposes that you will be serving only one wine with the entire meal – but even if you're planning multiple courses, each with a different wine, the main dish of the main course still stands as the central reference point: choose first the wine that will match with it, and then choose wines to lead up to it and, if you wish, away from it. That main dish and its wine and the harmonies or counterpoints they create provide the basic structure of your whole meal: Everything else flows from them.

For almost all occasions, ordinary or extraordinary, you will make your wine choice by a very simple process of matching components (or elements or characteristics: choose whichever term you like) of your main dish with similar ones in a wine. (Naturally, you can reverse the process too, and choose a main dish to match the characteristics of the wine you want.) Call it component-to-component matching: characteristic X in your food tells you look for a wine with matching characteristic X-1. It's as simple as that.

Wait a Minute

It's as simple as that, as long as you know which components of the food complement or are complemented by which components of the wine.

Some of them, like flavor intensity, suggest themselves at once. Under normal circumstances, balance is what you're seeking. Ideally, you want your wine and your food to be equally perceptible and equally enjoyable. There may be exceptions to this rule of thumb in some very special cases, but for most meals a genial parity between the intensity of the wine and food flavors is what you're after. Rules nine and ten above point precisely to this.

But foods have characteristics other than intensity. In fact, they even have different kinds of intensity: a dish can be intensely rich, or very sweet, or unbelievably hot, or markedly acidic. It can taste strongly of its basic ingredient – meat-sweet, or bell-pepper-sweet, or carrot-sweet, as opposed to sugar-sweet, or acidic from sauerkraut, or acidic in a different way from tomatoes or citrus fruits. Even delicate sensations can vary: the gently nutty flavor of crabmeat is immediately distinguishable from the bland mildness of chicken breasts or the succulent mildness of a creamy veal stew. That marvellous abundance of impressions that foods create on our palates, pleasurable though they all are, still causes anxiety for some people. The think that choosing wines to match with them demands an encyclopedic knowledge of every wine in the world – either that, or the whole process amounts to nothing more than blind luck.

Fortunately, neither of those extremes is the case. After you've made that very simple observation about strongly flavored dish vs. mildly flavored dish, and therefore strongly flavored wine vs. mildly flavored, your next task is merely to take note of the dominant flavor in the dish.

This deserves a bit more explanation. In most meals, whether plain or fancy, at home or dining out, one element usually dominates the meal, in the fundamental sense of being the flavor that calls most attention to itself or that characterizes the meal. If we broil a steak and serve it

with baked potato and green beans, the moist, beefy sweetness of the steak makes the palatal keynote of that dinner. If the baked potato and green beans accompany broiled scallops rather than steak, they still don't furnish the fundamental flavors of the meal: the gentle sea sweetness of the scallops provides the overall tone and character. Conversely, a good crabcake will taste predominantly of the gentle flavor of fresh crabmeat, while flaked crabmeat tossed with salad greens and dressed with strongly spiced dressing may well taste more of chili, garlic, or red pepper than of crab, and the clear palatal impression made by the whole ensemble may amount to a very assertively flavored dish, despite the crabmeat's intrinsic mildness.

Even a "composed" dish, one fashioned from many different ingredients, usually presents a single, definable character to the palate: A lamb stew, for instance, unifies meat and vegetables and broth into a single, moist and robust substantiality. A really fine bowl of chili may contain good beans and lean beef and maybe even tomato as well as onions and garlic, but what your palate notices are not the single voices of the individual ingredients but the harmony of them all that the spices bring about: a single, dominant palatal impression of spicy warmth. Whether the dish is humble stew or a glamorous civet, a down-home fry or sophisticated saute, that kind of dominant element is exactly what you have to spot and define or describe to yourself in order to choose a wine whose characteristics will mesh with it.

It may be helpful to think of this in terms of some simple dichotomies: Does the flavor of the basic ingredient dominate in the dish, or does the flavor of its condiments? And then, whichever dominates, is the flavor strong or mild? sweet or sour? Is the texture of the dish moist or dry? tender or chewy? Does the dish strike your taste buds as (choose one) rich? gelatinous? oily? pleasingly unctuous? or (choose one) austere? lean? dry? pleasingly fibrous? Each of those food characteristics has a counterpart in wine. Wines can be powerful or delicate, light or heavy, sweet or dry, fruity or acidic, soft on the palate or muscular and chewy, rich and mouth-filling or lean and austere.

While it helps a great deal to be aware of all these possibilities, you don't have to run through this whole gamut of oppositions for every wine and food you consider. Normally, the dominant characteristic of the food will either already be well known to you or it will leap right out at you. Moreover, the food characteristics that really matter boil down to a manageable few: the intensity or delicacy of the flavor; the nature of that flavor, which is usually a function of whether the base ingredients or its condiments dominate the preparation; and the balance of fats and acids in the dish (whether they come from the base or the condiments doesn't matter).

That last-named element is a crucial one: Fats and acids can make or break a food-and-wine match. The presence of fats in a dish at a palatally perceptible level dictates something important about the wine that will match well with it. A markedly acidic dish will scratch a "fat" wine to death (for example, spare ribs and sauerkraut will undo most Chardonnays) – but an acidic wine can make a very nice counterpoint to a rich and oily meal (Sauvignon blanc, for instance, works beautifully with deep-fried seafoods or rich sautes like sole or trout meuniere). Conversely: The leaner the dish, the fuller-bodied the wine it can respond to. This is because

the whole package of elements that make up what we perceive as a wine's body – alcohol and extract and acid and tannin and glycerine chiefly – often register on our palates as "fat." They can make us taste and feel a wine as heavy or oily or rich or greasy or buttery or any of dozens of other adjectives that people use in an attempt to surround and pin down this unmistakable, unverbalizable sensation.

Practical experience shows that a lean dish can support the complement of a "fat" wine, whereas a dish already rich and "fatty" will often make a rich wine seem excessive and heavy and overblown. So a roast chicken, say, or a simple veal cutlet could pair very successfully with a big, rich Chardonnay, while that same Chardonnay might very well taste flabby and heavy with a fried chicken. With the roast chicken, the wine's own body would be felt on the palate and tongue as a kind of fatness, in those circumstances pleasing and enjoyably lubricant. In combination with the fats of a fried dish, that same wine fatness can seem just too much, too overpowering of any other sensation the wine may offer. With the spare ribs and sauerkraut that I mentioned earlier, the Chardonnay's nicely composed flavor would come apart in the face of the acidity of the dish, and it would once again, though for a very different reason, taste flabby, as well as probably losing most of its fruit freshness.

Another Half a Decalogue

Here are some additional guidelines for partnering wine and food. Like the earlier ten comandments, these five all involve quite fundamental considerations about wine and food. You will find, as you go on to more and more complex food and wine matches, that the principles we're discussing here will still continue to operate, no matter how complicated the dining situations or sophisticated the wine choices. Which leads logically to the next principle:

11. The fundamentals of wine and food compatibility stay the same all across the spectrum of rarity and complexity, so all of the guides suggested in the decalogue (and those to be articulated below) remain valid in most if not all wine and food matchings, no matter how sophisticated the food preparation or how grand the wine.

12. In most cases the simplest form of a dish establishes its basic wine compatibilities, which most of the time are only refined, not transformed, by elaborations of the dish's presentation. This is truest of dishes built around strongly flavored basic ingredients; exceptions most often occur in the case of dishes that combine mildly flavored basic ingredients with markedly flavored condiments or seasonings.

13. Component-to-component matching – identifying the major flavors and characteristics of the food and the wine – is the key to even the most complex wine and food pairings, but not every component of every dish or every element in the wine has to be taken into account. In most cases, one or two dominant elements will cast the deciding votes.

14. Three characteristics of the main dish provide the basic factors that a wine must deal with to be genuinely compatible with that food: 1) intensity of flavor; 2) nature of the dominant flavor; 3) the ratio of fats to acid in the dish.

The perfect reflection of the winemaker's art.

WINERY LAKE CHARDONNAY • DIAMOND MOUNTAIN RANCH CHARDONNAY • WINERY LAKE PINOT NOIR
DIAMOND MOUNTAIN RANCH CABERNET SAUVIGNON • THREE PALMS VINEYARD RED TABLE WINE

VINEYARD DESIGNATED WINES

Three of Sterling's and Napa Valley's most famous vineyards — Winery Lake, Three Palms and Diamond Mountain Ranch — produce wines of such distinctive character that we are able to forego blending and, instead, bottle them individually and label them with the vineyard's name.

STERLING VINEYARDS®

15. The elements in wines that answer to those ingredients are 1) intensity of flavor, 2) kind of flavor, and 3) a conglomerate of elements that work to produce the total palatal effect of the wine: body and extract, tannin or acidity, and, in white wines, relative sweetness or dryness.

Once again, there is nothing mysterious or abstruse about any of this. To put it to use, however, you have to know a bit about the characteristics of different kinds of wines – the range of flavor intensity they present, the basic kinds of flavor they offer, and the nature of their own components, the bits and pieces that will let them work with a food's acids or fats. For every element in a food, there is a corresponding element in a wine: flavor, intensity, and texture all have their counterparts in the characteristics that make one wine a Barolo and another a white Burgundy. There are lots of books – mine among them – to help you learn the characteristics of the world's many wines, but there is no substitute for experience, for tasting a wine yourself and seeing how it registers on your palate, how it reacts to your favorite dinners. After all, the first truth about wine is also the last truth about wine: You taste only with your own mouth. So don't be shy about experimenting: try new wines, and new wine and food combinations. Find out what you like and why you like it, and then you can argue or agree with all the books that have ever been written about wine – or write your own, if you like.

---

*The material contained in this article is drawn from Tom Maresca's book, *The Right Wine: A User's Manual*, published by Grove-Weidenfeld and used here with the kind permission of Grove-Weidenfeld. A paperback edition of *The Right Wine* was released by Grove-Weidenfeld in 1992 along with a completely revised and updated version of Maresca's award-winning *Mastering Wine*.

The original edition of *Mastering Wine* was voted "Wine Book of the Year" in 1985. *The Right Wine* has been described as "a charming, chatty, and useful book": (Anthony Dias Blue), "a detailed manual for the lover of wine and food" (Gerald Boyd), "a fine job" (Robert Parker), "by far the most accessible guide to matching wine with food available today" and "a good read" (John Mariani). *The Wine Advocate* said succinctly "if you are serious about food and enjoy wine, this is the book for you."

A nationally known and internationally honored wine writer whose credits include *Attenzione, Food & Wine Magazine, Self, Town & Country, Ultra,* and *Wine & Spirits,* Maresca has also co-authored, with his wife, Diane Darrow, a book of Italian regional food and wine, *La Tavola Italiana* (William Morrow & Sons), and a book of Italian seasonal food and wine, *Seasons of the Italian Kitchen* to be published by Grove-Atlantic in Spring, 1994.

Because there are single malts.
And then there are the Classics.

Now Available In  The United States

Single Malt Scotch Whiskies: Talisker, 45.8% alc./vol.; Oban, 43% alc./vol.; Glenkinchie, 43% alc./vol.; Dalwhinnie, 43% alc./vol.; Lagavulin, 43% alc./vol.; Cragganmore, 40% alc./vol. Products of Scotland.

© Schieffelin & Somerset Co. New York, N.Y.

Gourmet Pantry

Chicken Stock

Ingredients

3 pounds chicken backs, wings, necks and bones, or a combination

14 1/2 cups cold water

2 onions, peeled and halved

2 whole cloves

4 unpeeled garlic cloves

1 celery rib, halved

2 carrots, halved

1 teaspoon salt

6 long parsley sprigs

12 black peppercorns

1/2 teaspoon dried thyme, crumbled

1 bay leaf

Preparation

If using wings, cut each wing at the joints into 3 pieces. In a stockpot or kettle, combine the chicken parts with 14 cups of cold water. Bring to a boil, skimming the froth, add the remaining 1/2 cup of cold water, and bring the mixture to a simmer, skimming the froth. Add the onions stuck with the cloves, the garlic, the celery, the carrots, the salt, the parsley, the peppercorns, the thyme, and the bay leaf and simmer the mixture, skimming the froth, for 3 hours. Strain the stock through a fine sieve into a bowl and let cool to warm.

If a more concentrated flavor is desired, boil the stock until it is reduced to the desired concentration. Chill the stock and remove the fat. The stock keeps, covered and chilled, for 1 week if it is brought to a boil every 2 days and then allowed to cool to warm, uncovered, before being chilled again, and keeps frozen, for 3 months. Makes about 10 cups.

Vegetable Stock

Ingredients

- 3 onions, chopped
- 3 tablespoons butter, unsalted
- The white and pale green part of 2 leeks, washed well and chopped
- 2 carrots, chopped
- 2 celery ribs, chopped
- 1/4 pound mushrooms (preferably ones with open caps)
- 1 cup potato peelings
- 12 1/3 cups cold water
- 1/4 cup lentils
- 6 unpeeled garlic cloves
- 1/2 teaspoon black peppercorns
- 1/2 teaspoon dried thyme, crumbled
- 1 bay leaf
- 12 long parsley sprigs
- 1 teaspoon salt

Preparation

In a stock pot or kettle, cook the onions in butter over moderate heat, stirring, until they are golden. Add the leeks, the carrots, the celery, the mushrooms, the potato peelings, and 1/3 cup of the water, and simmer the mixture, covered, stirring occasionally, for 5 minutes. Add the remaining water, the lentils, the garlic, the peppercorns, the thyme, the bay leaf, the parsley and the salt. Bring the mixture to a boil, and simmer it uncovered, for 2 hours.

Strain the stock through a fine sieve into a bowl and let it cool. Chill the stock and remove the fat.

Makes about 9 cups.

Fish Stock

Ingredients

1 pound of bones and trimmings of any white fish such as sole, flounder, or whiting, chopped

1 cup onions, sliced

12 long parsley sprigs

2 tablespoons fresh lemon juice

1/2 teaspoon salt

3 1/2 cups cold water

1/2 cup dry white wine

Preparation

In a well-buttered heavy saucepan, combine the fish bones and trimmings, the onions, the parsley, the lemon juice and the salt and steam the mixture, covered, over moderately high heat for 5 minutes. Add the water and the wine, bring the liquid to a boil, skimming froth, and simmer the mixture 20 minutes.

Strain the stock through a fine sieve into a bowl, let it cool to warm, and chill it covered. The stock keeps, covered and chilled, for 1 week if it is brought to a boil every 2 days and then allowed to cool to warm, uncovered, before being chilled again. The stock keeps frozen for 3 months. Makes about 3 cups.

White Veal Stock

Ingredients

2 pounds meaty veal knuckles, sawed into 2" pieces

12 1/2 cups cold water

1 large onion stuck with 2 cloves

2 leeks, halved lengthwise and washed well

1 carrot

1 celery rib, halved

1 teaspoon salt

A cheesecloth bag containing:
  4 parsley sprigs
  1/2 teaspoon dried thyme
  1 bay leaf

Preparation

In a kettle, cover the veal knuckles with 12 cups of the water, bring the water to a boil, and skim the froth. Add the remaining 1/2 cup water, bring the stock to a simmer, and skim any froth. Add the onion, the leeks, the carrot, the celery, the salt, and the cheesecloth bag and simmer the stock, skimming the froth and adding boiling water if necessary to keep the ingredients barely covered, for 2 hours more.

Strain the stock through a fine sieve set over a bowl, pressing hard on the solids, and let it cool. Chill the stock and remove the fat. The stock may be frozen. Makes about 6 cups.

Brown Stock

Ingredients

3 pounds of veal or beef bones, sawed into 2" pieces

2 pounds stew beef, cut into 1 1/2" cubes

2 unpeeled onions, quartered

2 carrots, halved

16 1/2 cups cold water

2 celery ribs, halved

4 unpeeled garlic cloves

6 long parsley sprigs

1 teaspoon salt

1/2 teaspoon dried thyme, crumbled

1 bay leaf

Preparation

Spread the bones and beef in a flame-proof roasting pan and roast them in a pre-heated 400° F oven for 25 minutes. Add the onions and the carrots, roast the mixture, stirring once or twice, for 30 minutes more, or until it is browned well, and transfer it with a slotted spoon to a stock pot or kettle. Pour off any fat from the pan, add 2 cups of the water, and deglaze the pan over high heat, scraping up the brown bits. Add the liquid to the pot with 14 cups of the remaining water and bring the liquid to a boil, skimming the froth. Add the remaining 1/2 cup of water and bring the mixture to a simmer, skimming the froth. Add the celery, the garlic, the parsley, the salt, the thyme, and the bay leaf and simmer the mixture for 4 hours.

If a more concentrated flavor is desired, boil the stock to the desired concentration. Strain the stock through a fine sieve into a bowl and let it cool to warm. Chill the stock and remove the fat. The stock keeps, covered and chilled, for 1 week if it is brought to a boil every 2 days and then allowed to cool to warm, uncovered, before being chilled again. The stock keeps, frozen, for 3 months. Makes about 8 cups.

Venison Game Stock

Ingredients

3 pounds of venison, cut into 1 1/2" cubes

1 1/2 pounds venison bones, cracked

12 1/2 cups cold water

1 onion stuck with 3 cloves

2 carrots, scraped and sliced

1 turnip, peeled and sliced

3 leeks, the white part only, washed and sliced

3 parsley roots, scraped

2 teaspoons salt

1 bay leaf

6 sprigs each fresh parsley, thyme, basil and rosemary

6 bruised peppercorns

6 crushed juniper berries

Preparation

In a kettle, cover the venison and venison bones with 12 cups of the water, bring the water to a boil, and skim the froth. Add the remaining 1/2 cup water, bring the stock to a simmer, and skim any froth. Add the onion, the carrots, the turnip, the leeks, the parsley roots, the salt, the bay leaf, the herbs, the peppercorns and juniper berries and simmer the stock, skimming the froth and adding boiling water if necessary to keep the ingredients barely covered, for 2 hours more.

Strain the stock through a fine sieve set over a bowl, pressing hard on the solids, and let it cool. Chill the stock and remove the fat. The stock may be frozen. Makes about 6 cups.

Demi-Glace

Ingredients

6 cups brown stock

Preparation

In a large sauce pan, cook the stock over moderate heat until it is reduce to about 4 cups. Let the demi-glace cool, transfer it to small freezer containers, and store, covered, in a freezer.

To use demi-glace, dip a spoon in hot water and spoon out the desired amount. The demi-glace keeps, frozen, indefinitely. Make about 4 cups.

Court Bouillon

Ingredients

1 small onion stuck with 2 cloves	1/2 teaspoon salt
1 slice of lemon	4 peppercorns
The leafy part (about 1/2) of a celery stalk	1/2 bay leaf
2 parsley sprigs	4 cups cold water

Preparation

In a saucepan, combine the onion, the lemon, the celery, the parsley, the salt, the peppercorns, the bay leaf and the water. Bring the water to a boil and simmer the mixture for 15 minutes.

Strain the court bouillon through a fine sieve. Makes about 3 3/4 cups.

Melba Sauce

Ingredients

2 cups fresh raspberries, or 2, 10 ounce packages frozen raspberries in light syrup, thawed, including the syrup	1/2 cup red currant jelly
1/4 cup sugar, or to taste	1 tablespoon eau-de-vie de framboise, or to taste if desired

Preparation

In a saucepan, combine the raspberries, the sugar and the red currant jelly and bring the mixture to a boil over high heat, crushing the raspberries with the back of a spoon, and simmer it, stirring occasionally, for 15 minutes or until it is thickened. Force the mixture through a fine sieve into a bowl, pressing hard on the solids. Transfer the sauce to a pan, cleaned, and boil it stirring occasionally for 5 minutes, or until it is thickened to the desired consistency. Stir in the eau-de-vie de framboise and chill the sauce, covered for at least 2 hours before serving it. Makes about 1 1/3 cups.

Glace de Viande

Ingredients

8 cups brown stock

Preparation

In a large saucepan, cook the stock over moderate heat until it is reduced to about 2 cups and is syrupy. Let the glace de viande cool, transfer it to small freezer containers and store it, covered, in a freezer.

To use the glace de viande, dip a spoon in hot water and spoon our the desired amount. The glace de viande keeps, frozen, indefinitely. Makes about 2 cups.

Brown Sauce

Ingredients

3 tablespoons unsalted butter

1/4 cup all-purpose flour

3 cups brown stock

1/2 teaspoon salt

Black pepper to taste

Preparation

In a saucepan, melt the butter. Stir in the flour and cook the roux over low heat, stirring, for 3 minutes. Remove the pan from the heat and add the stock, in a stream, whisking vigorously until the mixture is smooth. Add the salt and the pepper and simmer the sauce, stirring for 10 to 15 minutes, or until it is thickened to the desired consistency.

Strain the sauce through a fine sieve into a bowl and keep covered with a buttered round of wax paper to prevent a skin from forming. Makes about 2 1/4 cups.

Veloute Sauce

Ingredients

1 tablespoon minced onion

3 tablespoons unsalted butter

1/4 cup all-purpose flour

3 cups white veal stock, chicken stock or white fish stock

1/4 teaspoon salt

White pepper to taste

Preparation

In a saucepan, cook the onion in the butter over moderate heat, stirring, until it is softened. Stir in the flour and cook the roux over low heat, stirring, for 3 minutes. Remove the pan from the heat and add the stock, in a stream, whisking vigorously until the mixture is smooth. Add the salt and the white pepper and simmer the sauce, stirring for 10 to 15 minutes, or until it is thickened to the desired consistency.

Strain the sauce through a fine sieve into a bowl and keep covered with a buttered round of wax paper to prevent a skin from forming. Makes about 2 1/4 cups.

Bechamel Sauce

Ingredients

1 tablespoon minced onion

3 tablespoons unsalted butter

1/4 cup all-purpose flour

3 cups milk

1/4 teaspoon salt

White pepper to taste

Preparation

In a saucepan cook the onion in the butter over moderately low heat, stirring, until it is softened. Stir in the flour and cook the roux, stirring, for 3 minutes. Add the milk in a stream, whisking vigorously until the mixture is thick and smooth, add the salt and the pepper, and simmer the sauce for 10 to 15 minutes, or until it is thickened to the desired consistency. Strain the sauce through a fine sieve into a bowl and cover the surface with a buttered round of wax paper to prevent a skin from forming. Makes about 2 1/4 cups.

Sugar Syrup

Ingredients

1 cup sugar   2 cups water

Preparation

In a saucepan, combine the sugar and the water and bring the mixture to a boil, stirring and washing down any sugar crystals clinging to the sides with a brush dipped in cold water, until the sugar is dissolved. Cook the syrup over moderate heat, undisturbed, for 5 minutes and let it cool. The syrup keeps, in a sealed jar and chilled, indefinitely. Makes about 2 1/2 cups.

Fine Bread Crumbs

Ingredients

1 pound loaf of homemade white bread, sliced

Preparation

Tear the bread slices into 1" pieces and grind them finely in batches in a food processor or blender. The crumbs keep in an airtight container, chilled, for 2 weeks and frozen for 6 months. Makes about 6 cups.

Scallop Quenelles

Ingredients

3/4 pound sea scallops, rinsed and patted dry

1/2 teaspoon salt

1/2 cup chilled heavy cream

Preparation

Discard the tough bit of muscle clinging to the side of each scallop if necessary and in a food processor pureé the scallops with the salt. With the motor running add the cream in a stream and blend the mixture until it is just smooth.

In a large deep skillet bring 1 1/2 inches of salted water to a simmer. Scoop out and form ovals of the mousse with 2 soup spoons dipped in cold water, dropping each mound as it is formed into the simmering water, and poach the quenelles at a bare simmer, turning occasionally, for 6 minutes, or until they are springy to the touch. Transfer the quenelles with a slotted spoon to paper towels, let them drain briefly, and divide them between 2 heated plates.

Food Processor Dough

Ingredients

2 cups all-purpose flour

2 large eggs, beaten lightly

1 tablespoon olive oil

Preparation

In a food processor blend the flour, the eggs, the oil, and 2 tablespoons of water until the mixture just begins to form a ball, adding more water drip by drop if the dough is too dry, (the dough should be firm and not sticky). Blend the dough for 15 seconds more to knead it. (The dough may be prepared up to this point and kept covered and chilled up to 4 hours.) Let the dough stand, covered with an inverted bowl, at room temperature for 1 hour. Makes 1 pound.

To Roll Pasta Dough

Preparation

Set the smooth rollers of a pasta machine at the highest number. (The rollers will be wide apart.) Divide a pound of food processor pasta dough into 6 pieces, flatten 1 piece into a rough rectangle, and cover the remaining pieces with an inverted bowl. Dust the rectangle with flour and feed it through the rollers. Fold the rectangle in half and feed it through the roller 8 or 9 more times, folding it in half and dusting it with flour if necessary to prevent it from sticking. Turn the dial down one notch and feed the dough through the rollers without folding. Continue to feed the dough through the rollers without folding, turning the dial down one notch lower each time, until the lowest or second lowest notch is reached. The pasta dough should be a smooth long sheet about 4 to 5 inches wide and about 1/16" thick. Roll the remaining pasta dough in the same manner.

To Make Ravioli

Preparation

Make the ravioli: Roll out the dough as thin as possible on a pasta machine, following the procedure on the previous page but rolling and making the ravioli with 1 sheet of dough at a time. Trim the ends of the dough and cut the dough crosswise into 2 pieces, 1 piece 1 1/2" longer than the other. Put rounded teaspoons of the filling mixture in 2 rows on the shorter piece, spacing them about 1" from the edges and with their centers about 1 1/2" apart. Brush the dough around the filling with water, put the longer piece of the dough on top and press gently around the mounds of filling. With a fluted pastry wheel or knife cut the dough between the rows of filling into about 2" squares. Arrange the ravioli as they are formed in one layer on a lightly floured tray. Continue to make the ravioli, 1 sheet of dough at a time, with the remaining dough and filling in the same manner. The ravioli may be kept, uncovered and chilled, for up to 2 hours.

To Roast Bell Peppers

Preparation

Put the bell peppers on the rack of a broiler pan under a preheated broiler about 4" from the heat, turning them frequently, for 20 to 25 minutes, or until they are blistered and charred. Enclose the peppers in a paper bag and let them steam until they are cool enough to handle. Peel the peppers, starting at stem end, and discard the stems, the ribs and the seeds.

Clarified Butter

Ingredients

2 sticks, (1 cup) unsalted butter, cut into 1" pieces

Preparation

In a heavy saucepan melt the butter over low heat. Remove the pan from the heat, let the butter stand for 3 minutes, and skim the froth. Strain the butter into a bowl using a fine sieve made of a double thickness of rinsed and squeezed cheesecloth. Leave the milky solids in the bottom of the pan. Pour the clarified butter into a jar or crock and store it, covered, in the refrigerator. The butter keeps indefinitely, covered and chilled.

When clarified, butter loses about one fourth of its original volume. Makes about 3/4 cup.

Restaurants by Cuisine

American
The Frog and The Peach	60
Girafe	64
Highlawn Pavilion	70
The Inn at Millrace Pond	80
Ram's Head Inn	110

American/Contemporary
The Bernards Inn	30
Braddock's Tavern	36
Creations Restaurant & Meeting Place	40
Dennis Foy's Townsquare	44
The Dining Room at The Hilton at Short Hills	48
The Ebbitt Room	50
40 Main Street	56
Ken Marcotte	82
Washington Inn	128

American/Continental
Black Horse Inn	34
Llewellyn Farms	100
The Manor	102
Old Mill Inn	106
Rod's 1890's Restaurant	112

American/Seafood
Axelsson's Blue Claw Restaurant	24
Knife and Fork Inn	84

American/Steakhouse
Sammy's Ye Old Cider Mill	118

Chinese
Four Seas, Cuisines of China	58
Sing Ya	122

French
Beau Rivage	26
Fromagerie	62
L'Affaire 22	88
Le Papillon	98
The Ryland Inn	116

French/Contemporary
The Grand Cafe	66
Lahiere's	92

German/Continetal
Black Forest Inn	32

Italian
Benito Ristorante	28
Chateau Silvana	38
Cucina di Roma	42
Diamond's	46
Eccola Italian Bistro	52
The Farmingdale House	54
Harlequin Cafe	68
Il Capriccio	74
Il Tulipano	76
Il Villino	78
La Cucina Ristorante & Cafe	86
La Gondola	90
L'Allegria	94
Lantana	96
Mattar's	104
Panico's	108
Rudolfo Ristorante	114
Sestri Caffe & Ristorante	120
Valentino's	124
Villa Amalfi	126

Spanish/Portuguese
Iberia Peninsula	72

Swiss/Continental
Auberge Swiss	22

Recipes

Breads and Sauces

Bechamel Sauce	153
Gourmet Pantry	
Brown Sauce	152
Gourmet Pantry	
Clarified Butter	157
Gourmet Pantry	
Demi-Glace	150
Gourmet Pantry	
Fine Bread Crumbs	154
Gourmet Pantry	
Garlic Bread Formaggio	47
Diamond's	
Glace de Viande	152
Gourmet Pantry	
Melba Sauce	151
Gourmet Pantry	
Mustard Sauce	119
Sammy's Ye Old Cider Mill	
Sugar Syrup	154
Gourmet Pantry	
Veloute Sauce	153
Gourmet Pantry	

Desserts and Pastries

Charlotte Beau Rivage	27
Beau Rivage	
Chocolate Hazelnut Cake	83
Ken Marcotte	
Semi Freddo	79
Il Villino	

Fish and Shellfish

Baked Stuffed Prawns Llewellyn	101
Llewellyn Farms	
Cape May Monkfish with Horseradish Crust and Mustard Sauce	129
Washington Inn	
Chilled Tiger Prawns with Fava Bean Salad, Spicy Citrus Vinaigrette	49
The Dining Room at the Hilton at Short Hills	
Crabcakes	107
Old Mill Inn	
Gamberi Luciana	55
The Farmingdale House	
Grilled Shrimp with Salsa and Sweet Potato Chips	57
40 Main Street	
Knife & Fork Bouillabaisse	85
Knife & Fork Inn	
Lobster Cantonese Style	123
Sing Ya	
Lobster Terrine	37
Braddock's Tavern	
Pan Seared Tuna Steak in a Sesame Crust with Oriental Vegetables and a Spicy Thai Chili Salsa	41
Creations Restaurant & Meeting Place	
Rainbow Trout in a Hazelnut Crust	51
The Ebbitt Room	
Red Snapper alla Rudolfo	115
Rudolfo Ristorante	
Red Snapper and Shellfish Matelote	63
Fromagerie	
Salmone Farcito con Zucchini alla Menta	95
L'Allegria	
Scallop Quenelles	155
Gourmet Pantry	
Scallops Stuffed with Lobster Mousse, Champagne Sauce	103
The Manor	
Seafood Quenelles in Champagne Sauce	33
Black Forest Inn	
Sole Pignolia	109
Panico's	
Striped Bass with an Artichoke Crust	71
Highlawn Pavilion	

Meat and Poultry

Bistecca Nordestino	69
Harlequin Cafe	
Carne de Porco a Alentejana	73
Iberia Peninsula	
Chicken Giovanni	105
Mattar's	
Fettine Margherita	77
Il Tulipano	

Filetto di Bue al Gorgonzola	75	Fusilli with Vodka and Caviar	127
Il Capriccio		*Villa Amalfi*	
Filetto di Vitello al Tartufo Nero	91	Pappardelle Taormina	53
La Gondola		*Eccola Italian Bistro*	
Jade Chicken	59	Penne Bisanzio	125
Four Seas, Cuisines of China		*Valentino's*	
Pilgrim Creamy Chicken Pot Pie	111	Ravioli alla Ortalana	87
Ram's Head Inn		*La Cucina Ristorante & Cafe*	
Pollo Sestrino	121	Ravioli Piemontese	29
Sestri Caffe & Ristorante		*Benito Ristorante*	
Rack of Lamb, Prisille	113	To Make Ravioli	156
Rod's 1890's Restaurant		*Gourmet Pantry*	
Rack of Lamb with Bayaldi	93	To Roll Pasta Dough	156
Lahiere's		*Gourmet Pantry*	
Red Bank Veal Chop Calabrese	43		
Cucina di Roma			

Soups

Rillettes Le Papillon	99	
Le Papillon		
		Black Bean Soup with Andouille Sausage	65

		Girafe	
Roast Breast of Duck Finished with a Cranberry/Currant/Grand Marnier Demi-Glace	81	Broeto – Venetian Fish Soup	39
		Chateau Silvana	
		Brown Stock	149
The Inn at Millrace Pond		*Gourmet Pantry*	
Roast Chicken with Roasted Vegetables	117	Chicken Stock	145
The Ryland Inn		*Gourmet Pantry*	
Roasted Venison, Spaghetti Squash, Cranberries	45	Court Bouillon	151
		Gourmet Pantry	
Dennis Foy's Townsquare		Fish Stock	147
Roast Loin of Veal with Sweetbread Mousse	97	*Gourmet Pantry*	
Lantana		Vegetable Stock	146
Sautéed Quail Breast and Leg Dumplings with Rhubarb Black Currant Compoté	61	*Gourmet Pantry*	
		Venison Game Stock	150
The Frog and The Peach		*Gourmet Pantry*	
Sirloin Steak au Poivre	89	White Veal Stock	148
L'Affaire 22		*Gourmet Pantry*	
Veal Zurich	23	Wild Mushroom Soup	31
Auberge Swiss		*The Bernards Inn*	
		Wisconsin Cheddar and Crab Bisque	25
		Axelsson's Blue Claw Restaurant	

Pastas and Dumplings

Vegetables and Salads

Crispy Goat Cheese Dumplings with Mediterranean Style Vinaigrette	67	Roasted Tomato and Grilled Scallops over Mesclun Salad	35
The Grand Cafe		*Black Horse Inn*	
Food Processor Dough	155	To Roast Bell Peppers	157
Gourmet Pantry		*Gourmet Pantry*	

The restaurants in this guide are dedicated to providing total quality dining that consistently surpasses patrons' expectations.

To assure meeting these objectives, a total quality management program has been designed requiring valid feedback from anonymous auditors who volunteer to appraise the quality of dining experiences.

If you wish to be a volunteer restaurant auditor, please fill out and return this postcard.

Name _____

Address _____

City _____

State _____ Zip _____

1. How frequently do you dine out?
   ❏ Weekly   ❏ Monthly

2. Have you dined at any of the restaurants in the guide?
   ❏ Yes   ❏ No

3. If so, please list.
   _____
   _____
   _____

Please let us know of other recommendations you may have for full-service New Jersey restaurants, (allowed to serve wine with food), so that we may consider them for future guides.

_____
_____
_____
_____

Society of Quality Restaurants of New Jersey
5 Wessman Drive
West Orange, New Jersey 07052

Place Stamp Here